# ENOCH THE MAN WHO NEVER DIED

## Living A Life That Pleases God

Dr Michael H Yeager

All rights reserved. No part of this book is allowed to be reproduced, stored in a retrieval system, or transmitted by any form or by any means-electronic, mechanical, photocopy, recording, or otherwise-without prior written permission of the copyright owner, except by a reviewer who wishes to quote brief passages in connection with a review for inclusion in a magazine, website, newspaper, podcast, or broadcast. All Scripture quotations, unless otherwise indicated, are taken from the King James Authorized Version of the Bible.

**This book contains some information from public sources found online, but most of it is based on the author's real-life teachings and experiences.**

Copyright © 2024 Dr Michael H Yeager

All rights reserved.

ISBN: 9798338910627

## DEDICATION

To those who yearn, who are genuinely hungry and thirsty to live in the realm of the supernatural, this book is for you. To those who have already tasted the glories of the heavenly realm, this is dedicated to you. To the bride of Jesus Christ, who is called to delve deeper, to soar higher, and to journey farther than ever before, this dedication stands as a **Testament**. It is only by the unmerited grace of our Lord, obtained through unwavering FAITH in JESUS CHRIST, that we can hope to achieve His divine will on this earth. As we face the adversary, Satan, and the powers of darkness, may we always remember our purpose and calling.

# CONTENTS

# ACKNOWLEDGMENTS

| 1 | Chapter One | 1 |
| 2 | Chapter Two | 21 |
| 3 | Chapter Three | 39 |
| 4 | Chapter Four | 58 |
| 5 | Chapter Five | 73 |
| 6 | Chapter Six | 90 |
| 7 | Chapter Seven | 109 |
| 8 | Chapter Eight | 128 |
| 9 | Chapter Nine | 145 |
| 10 | Chapter Ten | 164 |

# ACKNOWLEDGMENTS

*To our heavenly Father and His wonderful love.

*To our Lord, Savior and Master — **Jesus Christ**, who saved us and set us free because of His great love for us.

*To the Holy Spirit, who leads and guides us into the realm of truth and miraculous living every day.

*To all of those who had a part in helping me get this book ready for the publishers.

*To my Lovely Wife, and our precious children, Michael, Daniel, Steven, Stephanie, Catherine Yu, who is our precious daughter-in-law, and Naomi, who is now with the Lord.

# **Important Introduction**

The stories that I have witnessed, experienced, and shared within this book are all true events that have occurred in my life, my family's life, and the lives of others. I have recounted these stories of healing to the best of my ability, aiming to convey the truth of each miraculous event.

It is important to note that the stories included here do not encompass every healing, miracle, or blessing we have experienced. If I were to document every answered prayer and every divine intervention, this book would be endless!

In this book, I am going to share some of the most significant moments we have witnessed in our walk with the Lord. Some of these accounts may seem unbelievable, but I assure you, they are genuine. This is not a testament to our own spirituality, but rather a celebration of the wonderful and marvelous works of the Father, the Son, and the Holy Ghost.

As I recount these incredible experiences, please understand that not every dialogue is recalled verbatim, but each story is shared with as much accuracy as possible. Additionally, due to privacy considerations, I am unable to name everyone involved in these events. If you recognize an experience or were a part of one of these moments, know that while your name is not mentioned, your role in these stories is greatly valued and appreciated. Please do not feel overlooked or forgotten.

# CHAPTER ONE

## **Enoch: The Man Taken by God – Unveiling a Life of Divine Favor**

---

Enoch is one of the most mysterious and inspiring figures in the Bible, known for living a life so faithful to God that he was taken directly to heaven without experiencing death. Enoch, the great-grandson of Adam and the great-grandfather of Noah, is a man whose life demonstrates the power of walking closely with the Creator. He fathered Methuselah, the longest-living person in the Bible, and is remembered for his holy and devoted life, spanning over 300 years.

The name "Enoch" holds significant meaning, translating to "teaching" or "instruction." His life, filled with divine purpose, was part of God's plan, pointing toward the coming of Jesus Christ. The meanings of the names from Adam to Noah form a prophetic message of salvation, with Enoch's role as a key figure in this lineage.

In this book, we delve into Enoch's extraordinary life, exploring his legacy as one of only two individuals in Scripture who were taken up to heaven without dying—

the other being the prophet Elijah. Through biblical insights and fascinating connections to the coming Messiah, *Enoch: The Man Taken by God* sheds light on how Enoch's walk with God is a model for every believer.

Join us as we examine his role in the divine plan and how his life points to the ultimate hope and comfort found in Jesus Christ.
Enoch's story, though brief in Scripture, holds profound lessons about faith, obedience, and walking in unbroken fellowship with God. While much of the biblical narrative provides us with details of his lineage and his close relationship with the Lord, Enoch's impact echoes through the ages. His life was not marked by extraordinary feats, but by his unwavering faithfulness, which pleased God so much that he was spared the natural process of death.

In this book, we also explore the significance of Enoch's name and the prophetic meanings hidden within the genealogies of his time. From Adam to Noah, each name tells a part of the redemptive story, and Enoch's name—meaning "teaching"—points to the ultimate revelation of God's plan through Jesus Christ. Enoch's walk with God is a shadow of the greater walk that Jesus would later fulfill.

We will also discuss the *Pseudepigrapha*, particularly the *Book of Enoch*, an ancient text that, while not included in the biblical canon, has sparked much intrigue over the centuries. The *Book of Enoch* offers additional insights into his life, his role as a prophet, and his visions of heaven, although these accounts should be read with discernment. Personally I do not embrace this book as being authentic because there are many statements and teachings that are contradictory to the Bible.

## THE BOOK YOU HOLD IN YOUR HANDS

By uncovering the depths of Enoch's life, his walk with God, and his prophetic significance, this book aims to inspire readers to pursue their own close relationship with the Lord. Just as Enoch walked faithfully with God and was taken into His presence, we too are invited to walk daily with our Creator, trusting in His promises and living lives that please Him.

*Enoch: The Man Taken by God – Unveiling a Life of Divine Favor* is more than just a story about a man who never died; it is a call to walk in faith, to seek God wholeheartedly, and to live with the hope of eternal communion with Him. Through Enoch's example, we see the rewards of a life lived in complete surrender to God—a life that ultimately leads to the divine embrace of heaven.

---

## **Enoch and the Mystery of the Rapture: Unraveling the End Times Through the Life of God's Faithful Servant**

---

The story of Enoch, a man who was taken directly to

heaven without experiencing death, remains one of the most intriguing events in biblical history. But how does this extraordinary event relate to the broader narrative of faith, and why is it important to us today? In this comprehensive exploration, we will dive into the biblical account of Enoch and the extra-biblical traditions surrounding his life, specifically the pseudonymous *Book of Enoch*.

We begin by examining the significance of Enoch's translation to heaven as a symbol of the future rapture—a moment when God will snatch believers away at the end of times, as depicted in **Thessalonians 4:16-17**. How does Enoch's escape from death serve as a precursor to this event? What can his story teach us about living faithfully in a morally depraved world?

We'll also analyze why Enoch was chosen for this unique departure while other great heroes of faith in Hebrews 11, like Noah and Abraham, had to face death. As the world grows increasingly wicked, parallels between Enoch's time and the coming apocalypse are striking. The faith of Enoch, like Elijah after him, serves as a model for believers living in the face of overwhelming opposition.

Additionally, this book will touch on the often-debated *Book of Enoch*—a non-canonical text that delves into apocalyptic themes, angels, the Nephilim, and the fate of the wicked. While not part of the accepted biblical canon, the *Book of Enoch* has fascinated scholars and Christians alike, with some passages appearing to be referenced in Jude and 2 Peter.

*Enoch and the Mystery of the Rapture* unpacks these complex themes, weaving together the biblical story, prophetic visions, and end-times theology. Through this lens, we learn that Enoch's story is not merely ancient history, but a glimpse into the future for believers. Whether we face death or live to witness the rapture, Enoch's walk with God provides hope and a path of faithfulness in the days ahead.

Enoch's journey is more than just a miraculous event of being taken by God—it serves as a profound symbol of the hope and promise that believers cling to as we anticipate the return of Christ. In *Enoch and the Mystery of the Rapture*, we delve deeper into the significance of this enigmatic figure and how his life provides a blueprint for Christians living in today's world.

The question of *why* Enoch was spared death when even other faithful heroes like Abraham, Moses, and David faced it raises important theological reflections. The Bible offers no explicit reason, but his unwavering walk with God is a strong indication of what pleases the Lord. Enoch's story suggests that a life lived in close communion with God, one that is lived by faith can lead to divine favor, making him an example for us today as we strive to navigate a fallen world. Enoch's life was marked not by grand miracles or great achievements, but by his quiet faithfulness—an extraordinary walk that brought him into the very presence of God.

In addition to this, we will explore the broader

eschatological implications of Enoch's translation. Some theologians view Enoch's experience as a foreshadowing of the rapture—a moment described in **1 Thessalonians 4:16-17,** when Christ will return, and believers will be **"caught up"** to meet Him in the air. Enoch's journey from earth to heaven without experiencing death mirrors this event, serving as a symbolic precursor of what is to come for those who remain faithful.

As we further examine the *Book of Enoch*, which many early Jewish and Christian traditions respected, we'll uncover its rich apocalyptic themes. The *Book of Enoch* offers vivid descriptions of the heavenly realm, angelic beings, and divine judgment on the wicked. While not part of the biblical canon, this text influenced much of early Christian eschatology and provides fascinating context for understanding Enoch's role in the divine plan. Jude's epistle, for instance, appears to quote directly from this text, lending weight to its insights on Enoch's prophetic authority.

However, the focus of this book remains squarely on what Scripture reveals: Enoch's steadfastness and devotion to God in the midst of a corrupt world, much like our own. His story reminds us that while the world may descend into chaos and moral decay, walking with God ensures a path of safety and ultimate deliverance. The parallels between Enoch's time and our own are too striking to ignore. As believers today grapple with an increasingly hostile world, Enoch's faithfulness serves as a model for living in holiness and trust in God's promises.

*Enoch and the Mystery of the Rapture* challenges readers to consider their own walk with God. Are we living in such a way that we, too, would be counted as righteous in the eyes of the Lord? As we navigate our own trials and temptations, Enoch's life stands as a beacon of hope, reminding us that God rewards those who earnestly seek Him.

Whether you're interested in biblical history, end-times prophecy, or deepening your faith, this book offers a unique perspective on one of the Bible's most mysterious figures. Enoch's life, though brief in Scripture, holds timeless truths for every believer, providing a glimpse into the future that awaits those who live in faithfulness to God.

## **Unveiling the Dark Powers: The Occult, Angelic Language, and the Heresies of John Dee and Edward Kelly**

---

Throughout history, the unseen forces of the spiritual realm have fascinated and haunted mankind. This book delves in a minor extent into the unsettling world of 16th-century occultists John Dee and Edward Kelly, who claimed to have unlocked an angelic language, *Enochian*, which allowed them to communicate with supernatural beings. Known for their diaries and rituals involving a black obsidian mirror and a crystal ball, Dee and Kelly believed they had access to a celestial discourse that gave them insight into hidden knowledge and even superhuman powers.

Their mysterious practices were rooted in the belief that this ancient language, which they referred to as the "first language of God and Christ," was last known by the biblical patriarch Enoch. This belief fueled their pursuit of the occult, which they claimed would reshape Europe's political structure and herald the end times.

In this shallow exploration, we uncover the dark influence of demonic powers at work in these rituals, along with the historical and spiritual implications of their heresies. From the complex grammar of the *Enochian* language to the angels' warnings of apocalypse, this book examines the evidence of demonic deception in Dee and Kelly's work and their lasting impact on occult practices today.

The Bible paints a very different picture of Enoch, the man who walked with God and was taken to heaven without seeing death. Through the contrast of Enoch's righteousness with the false claims surrounding the *Enochian* language, this book reveals the stark divide between true divine communication and the dangers of engaging with occult forces.

Prepare to uncover the truth behind John Dee and Edward Kelly's heresies, and the evidence of demonic powers at work in our world today.

## **The Two Enochs: A Tale of

# Wickedness and Righteousness in Biblical Lineage**

---

Before diving into the remarkable story of Enoch who was taken by God, it's crucial to recognize that the Bible mentions two distinct individuals named Enoch. The first Enoch, Cain's eldest son, came from a wicked lineage. The Bible tells us that this Enoch had a city named after him by his father, symbolizing his place in the ungodly lineage of Cain.

In contrast, the second Enoch belonged to the righteous lineage of Seth, Adam's third son. This Enoch, the son of Jared, became known for his extraordinary relationship with God. He walked so closely with the Creator that he was taken up to heaven without experiencing death, a privilege shared by only one other person in the Bible—Elijah. This Enoch, from the line that preserved the knowledge of God, is also known as the father of Methuselah, the man who lived the longest in human history, reaching 969 years.

However, Methuselah was not Enoch's only child. The Bible mentions that Enoch had other sons and daughters, though their names are not recorded. What distinguishes this Enoch is his deep relationship with God, signified by the phrase "Enoch walked with God." Interestingly, this expression is only used in the Bible to describe Enoch and Noah, Enoch's great-grandson, highlighting their special bond with the Lord.

Enoch lived 365 years, a lifespan that some scholars suggest may symbolically correspond to the days of a solar year, representing a life of completeness and favor. However, this interpretation remains debated, as Genesis 5 primarily presents genealogical records, which are not typically interpreted symbolically.

The Bible explores the lives of these two Enochs—their contrasting lineages, legacies, and what their stories reveal about walking with or against God. While one Enoch is remembered for building a city, the other is remembered for his intimate walk with the Creator, culminating in his divine translation to heaven.

---

## ** Enoch and the Mystery of Divine Translation: A Life with God Beyond Death**

---

The story of Enoch, a man taken directly into the presence of God without experiencing death, stands as a fascinating mystery in the biblical narrative. His life, though shorter than most pre-flood patriarchs, is filled with significance and spiritual depth. While his son Methuselah holds the record for the longest lifespan in the Bible, it is Enoch's unique communion with God that elevates him to a place of unmatched privilege—being taken bodily into heaven.

This book explores the profound details of Enoch's life and the discussions surrounding his mysterious departure from the earth. Was Enoch's 365 years a symbolic number, or should we, like other biblical ages, take it literally? If understood literally, Enoch lived the shortest life among the patriarchs, yet his early departure was far from a tragedy. Instead, it marked an extraordinary elevation to eternal fellowship with God—an experience that transcends the value of mere longevity.

Jewish traditions and biblical interpreters have long debated whether the statement "God took Enoch" was simply a poetic reference to the death of a righteous man. However, within Christianity, the prevailing interpretation is clear: Enoch did not see death. The writer of Hebrews supports this, saying, **"By faith Enoch was translated that he should not see death" (Hebrews 11:5).** For those who believe in the full inspiration and inerrancy of the Bible, this translation was a real, physical event that set Enoch apart, along with the prophet Elijah, as one of the only two Old Testament figures to bypass death.

This book delves into the significance of Enoch's walk with God, the theological implications of his translation, and the parallels with other figures like Noah and Elijah. What does Enoch's life teach us about the power of faith, the privilege of divine communion, and the hope of eternal life? As we examine the biblical texts and interpretations surrounding Enoch, we uncover timeless truths about living a life that pleases God and what it means to walk closely with Him.

# **Enoch's Journey: Immortality,

Dr Michael H Yeager

# Faith, and the Apocryphal Debate**

---

Enoch's story has long captivated readers of the Bible, offering a glimpse into the mystery of a natural man walking with God so closely that he was taken to heaven without tasting death. His life, immortalized in Genesis, Hebrews, and Jude, also presents key insights into the concept of immortality and the role of faith in pleasing God. But beyond the biblical text, Enoch's legacy has sparked considerable debate, especially concerning the apocryphal *Book of Enoch* and its influence on early Christian thought.

Enoch's role in the genealogy of Jesus, as noted in Luke, and his mention in Hebrews 11 as one of the heroes of faith emphasize his significance in the biblical narrative. The Bible describes Enoch's faith as so powerful that it led to his being "taken away" by God, sparing him from death. Jude further references Enoch in a prophecy about divine judgment upon the wicked. Scholars often debate whether Jude's citation came from the apocryphal *Book of Enoch* or from an earlier oral tradition, adding a layer of intrigue to Enoch's story.

The apocryphal writings attributed to Enoch, most notably *The First Book of Enoch*, have sparked interest and controversy alike. While the Bible contains 66 books that many Christians, including the author, consider more than sufficient for faith and practice, *The Book of Enoch* offers extra-biblical accounts of angels, fallen beings, and end-times prophecies. Scholars agree that these writings likely date back to 200 BC to the first century AD, long after Enoch's lifetime, though some believe they contain remnants of oral traditions connected to Enoch himself.

Despite its non-canonical status, *The Book of Enoch* was known to early Christian figures such as Clement of Alexandria and Tertullian. However, its original Hebrew version was lost, and today only fragments in Greek and Ethiopian have survived. The debate around these texts continues, with some viewing them as historical artifacts that provide insight into early Jewish and Christian eschatology, while others question their value beyond scholarly curiosity. It could be that it is a mixture of truth and deception in that there are those who could have added their own ideology. This scenario is most likely the case.

This book explores Enoch's life as it pertains to what it means: He Walked with God! We will explore his role as a man of faith, and the theological significance of his translation into heaven.

Through Enoch's extraordinary story, we are invited to reflect on the themes of immortality, faith, and divine favor. What does it mean to walk so closely with God that death is not part of the equation?

To **"walk with God"** means to live a life in close relationship and constant fellowship with the Creator, aligning one's actions, thoughts, and desires with God's will. It represents a lifestyle of obedience, faith, and devotion to God, seeking His guidance in every aspect of life. This walk signifies living in harmony with God's principles, showing dependence on Him, and growing in spiritual maturity.

Here are some key elements of walking with God, supported by KJV scriptures:

1. **Living in Constant Fellowship with God**
Walking with God involves maintaining a continuous connection with Him through prayer, worship, and the study of His Word. Enoch is a prime example of this relationship.

*"**And Enoch walked with God: and he was not; for God took him.**"*
**(Genesis 5:24)**

2. **Faith and Trust in God's Guidance**
Walking with God requires unwavering faith in His plan and trusting Him even when circumstances seem uncertain. Enoch's faith was key to his walk with God.

*"**By faith Enoch was translated that he should not see death; and was not found, because God had translated him: for before his translation he had this testimony, that he pleased God.**"*
**(Hebrews 11:5)**

3. **Obedience to God's Commands**
To walk with God is to live in obedience to His commandments, striving to live a life that reflects His character and holiness. The Bible emphasizes the importance of walking in God's ways.

*"Ye shall walk after the LORD your God, and fear him, and keep his commandments, and obey his voice, and ye shall serve him, and cleave unto him."*
(Deuteronomy 13:4)

4. **Living in Righteousness**
Walking with God means pursuing righteousness, which involves rejecting sin and choosing to live according to God's standards. Noah, like Enoch, was also described as walking with God because of his righteousness.

*"These are the generations of Noah: Noah was a just man and perfect in his generations, and Noah walked with God."*
(Genesis 6:9)

5. **Humility and Dependence on God**
Walking with God requires humility, recognizing that we depend on God for wisdom, strength, and guidance. It means seeking His will in every aspect of life rather than relying on our own understanding.

*"He hath shewed thee, O man, what is good; and what doth the LORD require of thee, but to do justly, and to love mercy, and to walk humbly with thy God?"*
(Micah 6:8)

6. **Abiding in God's Presence**
When we walk with God, we remain in His presence, seeking His face daily and desiring closeness with Him. This results in peace, joy, and spiritual growth.

*"If we live in the Spirit, let us also walk in the Spirit."*
(Galatians 5:25)

7. **Seeking God's Will and Direction**
Walking with God means constantly seeking His will for our lives. This involves asking for His guidance in every decision and trusting Him to lead us on the right path.

*"Trust in the LORD with all thine heart; and lean not unto thine own understanding. In all thy ways acknowledge him, and he shall direct thy paths."*
(Proverbs 3:5-6)

8. **Walking in the Light of God's Truth**
Walking with God also implies walking in the light of His truth, living a life of honesty, integrity, and love, reflecting God's character in the world.

*"But if we walk in the light, as he is in the light, we have fellowship one with another, and the blood of Jesus Christ his Son cleanseth us from all sin."*
(1 John 1:7)

9. **Endurance and Perseverance**
Walking with God requires endurance, especially during trials and hardships. It means persevering in faith and remaining steadfast in the Lord, knowing that He is with us every step of the way.

*"And let us not be weary in well doing: for in due season we shall reap, if we faint not."*

**(Galatians 6:9)**

**Summary:**
Walking with God is a lifelong journey of faith, obedience, and reliance on Him. It means staying close to God, seeking His presence, and allowing His Spirit to guide our every step. Those who walk with God, like Enoch and Noah, set an example of what it means to live a life fully committed to the Lord, pleasing Him in all things.

# Yes Sir, No Sir

From a young age, my father ingrained in all of us the practice of responding with "Yes Sir" and "No Sir." This became so much a part of who we were that even well into my 30s, this was how I naturally spoke to him. It wasn't just a simple habit; it was a reflection of our deep respect for authority. Much of this discipline can be attributed to our family's military background. Both of my brothers, Dennis and Dan, served in the Army. My sister, Debbie, joined the Air Force, and I served in the Navy. My father had been both Air Force and Navy, while his older brother, my Uncle Gilbert, retired from the Air Force.

Looking back, I see how this upbringing has influenced my walk with Christ. Being taught to respect authority instilled in me a profound understanding of obedience. I can't recall a single instance where I ever back-talked my father. While we didn't always see eye-to-eye, I never disrespected him. This concept seems foreign in today's society, where the reverence for authority is often lost.

I believe this lack of respect for authority is part of why there is such a deficit of faith in the body of Christ today. Consider the centurion in the Bible, a man who understood authority so deeply that it amazed Jesus. When the centurion needed a miracle, he told Jesus, *"**Lord, I am not worthy that thou shouldest come under my roof: but speak the word only, and my servant shall be healed" (Matthew 8:8, KJV).*** He understood the power of authority, saying, *"**For I am a man under authority, having soldiers under me: and I say to this man, Go, and he goeth; and to another, Come, and he cometh" (Matthew 8:9, KJV).*** Jesus marveled at his faith, declaring, *"**Verily I say unto you, I have not found so great faith, no, not in Israel" (Matthew 8:10, KJV).***

This profound faith, born out of a recognition of authority, is what God seeks from us. He is looking for those whose response to His Word is, "Yes Sir," or "No Sir," without hesitation or doubt. This is the kind of obedience that moves mountains and sees miracles. When we yield fully to God's authority, trusting Him completely, we unlock the power of faith that transforms lives.

God calls us to walk in this kind of submission, just as Jesus did when He said, *"**Nevertheless not my will, but thine, be done" (Luke 22:42, KJV).*** This is the heart of a servant, the heart that says, "Yes Sir" to God's will, trusting in His perfect plan.

Enoch The Man Who Never Died

# CHAPTER TWO
## ** Living by Faith, Not by Works – Lessons from the Life of Enoch**

---

**Hebrews 11:5-6** tells us, *"By faith Enoch was translated that he should not see death; and was not found, because God had translated him: for before his translation he had this testimony, that he pleased God. But without faith it is impossible to please him: for he that cometh to God must believe that he is, and that he is a rewarder of them that diligently seek him."*  This powerful scripture reveals how Enoch, through faith, bypassed death, becoming a living testament to the reward of those who earnestly seek God.

The writer of Hebrews reminds us of the enduring truth that faith that has works, not works alone, is the only path to reconciliation with God. Just as Enoch's faith pleased God and brought him into His eternal presence, so too must we place our trust in Him to walk a life that pleases the Lord.

Throughout generations, the Jewish people had been steeped in a corrupted form of Judaism, believing that they could earn their way to God through their own morality, works, or religious ceremonies with out true faith. But as **Romans 3:28** states, *****"Therefore we conclude that a man is justified by faith without the deeds of the law."***** The letter to the Hebrews served as a reminder that from the very beginning, faith has always been the means of salvation.

Enoch's story echoes the deeper message of salvation through faith alone. Much like Abel, who offered a blood sacrifice as a recognition of sin, Enoch lived a life that demonstrated the transformative power of walking closely with God. As we follow the example of Christ, who paid the ultimate sacrifice for our sins on the cross, we are reminded that our salvation rests solely in His grace, through faith.

**Ephesians 2:8 For by grace are ye saved through faith; and that not of yourselves: it is the gift of God: 9 Not of works, lest any man should boast.10 For we are his workmanship, created in Christ Jesus unto good works, which God hath before ordained that we should walk in them.**

By reflecting on the life of Enoch and these great heroes of faith, we can better understand the profound truth that, *****"The just shall live by faith" (Romans 1:17).***** Jesus Himself declared in **John 14:6,** *****"I am the way, the truth, and the life: no man cometh unto the Father, but by me."***** It is only through Jesus and our trust in His sacrifice that we can find eternal life and live a life that pleases God.

Enoch's life provides a vivid example of what it means to walk with God, living by faith and trusting in His promises. This walk is not based on human effort, religious rituals, or moral achievements but is grounded in faith—faith that transforms, sustains, and leads to eternal life. Enoch's translation into heaven, where he bypassed death, is a foreshadowing of the ultimate promise for those who place their trust in God through Jesus Christ.

As **Hebrews 11:5** reminds us, Enoch *"**was not found because God had taken him.**"* This mysterious and miraculous event demonstrates God's reward for those who diligently seek Him. Enoch's life was marked by his deep relationship with the Lord, a life of faith that pleased God so much that He chose to bring Enoch into His presence without experiencing physical death. This powerful imagery parallels the promise given to believers in **1 Thessalonians 4:16-17**, where we are told that Jesus will return, and *"**the dead in Christ shall rise first: Then we which are alive and remain shall be caught up together with them in the clouds, to meet the Lord in the air.**"*

Just as Enoch walked closely with God, we too are called to walk by faith in the footsteps of Jesus, who provided the perfect example of living in obedience to the Father. Jesus' sacrifice on the cross and His resurrection from the dead fulfilled the law, showing us that salvation is by grace through faith and not of works, as **Ephesians 2:8-9** teaches: *"**For by grace are ye saved through faith;**

**and that not of yourselves: it is the gift of God: Not of works, lest any man should boast."***

That is a works that is simply human endeavor. A persons own physical efforts with no looking to God for the strength to keep Gods laws!

Enoch's life underscores the reality that faith is the key to pleasing God. It is through faith that we are justified, sanctified, and ultimately glorified in Christ. The lives of the Old Testament heroes, including Enoch, were never about their own righteousness but about their trust in God's promises, which produced obedience. This truth has been consistent throughout Scripture, as **Romans 4:3** emphasizes: ***"For what saith the scripture? Abraham believed God, and it was counted unto him for righteousness."***

The story of Enoch serves as an encouragement for us today. Just as Enoch trusted in God's plan and walked with Him, we too are called to trust in Jesus Christ and live by faith. Our faith is not merely belief in the existence of God, but a personal, daily reliance on Him, trusting in His promises, His Word, and His ultimate plan for our lives.

Jesus said in **John 6:47**, ***"Verily, verily, I say unto you, He that believeth on me hath everlasting life."*** Through faith in Christ, we receive the gift of eternal life, and like Enoch, we will one day be in the presence of God, not because of our own works but because of the righteousness of Jesus credited to us by faith.

In conclusion, the life of Enoch offers a timeless reminder that faith is not only the foundation of our relationship with God but the key to living a life that pleases Him. As **Hebrews 11:6** says, *"**Without faith, it is impossible to please Him.**"* Let Enoch's story inspire us to walk closely with God, trusting fully in His Son, Jesus Christ, and looking forward to the day when we too will be caught up in His glorious presence for eternity.

# **Methuselah's Prophecy: Judgment Delayed by Grace**

---

The story of Methuselah and his father Enoch holds a profound message of God's judgment and grace. Methuselah's name itself was a prophecy—its meaning implied that his death would bring judgment. Methuselah, the man who lived longer than anyone else on Earth, became a living reminder of the impending flood, a judgment against the wickedness of humanity. **Genesis 5:27** says, *"**And all the days of Methuselah were nine hundred sixty and nine years: and he died.**"* His life spanned 969 years, a testament to God's incredible patience in delaying judgment.

God's grace is revealed in Methuselah's long life. For almost a millennium, the world was given time to repent. But the year Methuselah died, the floodwaters came. **Genesis 7:11** tells us, *"**In the six hundredth year of Noah's life, in the second month, the seventeenth day**"*

**of the month, the same day were all the fountains of the great deep broken up, and the windows of heaven were opened."\*** The long-suffering patience of God extended through Methuselah's life, but when he died, so came the judgment.

The story of Enoch, Methuselah's father, is equally remarkable. Enoch lived only 365 years, a much shorter lifespan compared to others of his era. Yet, Enoch is remembered not for how long he lived but for how he lived—he walked with God. **Genesis 5:24 says, \*"And Enoch walked with God: and he was not; for God took him."\*** Twice, in both verses 22 and 24, the Bible emphasizes that Enoch walked faithfully with God for 300 years, living a godly life in a world filled with corruption.

Enoch's faithfulness becomes even more significant when we consider the condition of the world he lived in. The Bible tells us that the earth was so corrupt that God regretted creating mankind. **Genesis 6:5 says, \*"And God saw that the wickedness of man was great in the earth, and that every imagination of the thoughts of his heart was only evil continually."\*** Enoch lived in a world consumed by sin, yet he stood apart, walking closely with God. His faith was so strong that he was taken up into heaven without experiencing death—a testimony to a life that pleased the Lord.

**This leads us to reflect on the question:** What would our own testimony be if we lived in such a corrupt world for 300 years? Could we remain faithful to God in the face of overwhelming sin? Could it be said of us, as it was of Enoch, that we walked so closely with God that we were spared death itself?

Enoch's story, along with Methuselah's prophetic life, reminds us of God's grace and patience, but also of His ultimate judgment. The flood came after Methuselah's death, but God extended mercy for nearly 1,000 years, allowing time for repentance. In the same way, **2 Peter 3:9** reminds us, ***"The Lord is not slack concerning his promise, as some men count slackness; but is longsuffering to us-ward, not willing that any should perish, but that all should come to repentance."***

And as Enoch walked with God, so are we called to walk with Him through faith in Jesus Christ, who offers us grace and redemption from judgment. **John 5:24** declares, ***"Verily, verily, I say unto you, He that heareth my word, and believeth on him that sent me, hath everlasting life, and shall not come into condemnation; but is passed from death unto life."*** Like Enoch, those who walk by faith in Christ will one day be taken into the eternal presence of God, escaping the ultimate judgment.

The lives of Enoch and Methuselah are a powerful reminder of God's grace, His call to faithfulness, and His promise of redemption through Jesus Christ. As we consider their stories, we are invited to examine our own walk with God and trust in the grace He extends through His Son.

## **Walking with God: A Life of Faith and

# Fellowship from Enoch to Abraham**

---

The story of Enoch's 300-year walk with God is a remarkable testimony to faithfulness and intimate communion with the Creator. As we reflect on his life, we are reminded of the profound relationship God desires to have with His people, not just in brief moments but over a lifetime. **Hebrews 11:5-6 says, *"By faith Enoch was translated that he should not see death; and was not found, because God had translated him: for before his translation he had this testimony, that he pleased God. But without faith it is impossible to please him."*** This scripture encapsulates the essence of Enoch's walk with God—he pleased the Lord through his faith.

The early years of human history, even before the flood, offer a spirituality that may surprise some. Far from the legalistic approach that many associate with the Old Testament, these ancient stories emphasize the closeness of walking with God. This was not about mere obedience to a distant and demanding deity; it was about intimate fellowship. Just as Adam and Eve walked and talked with God in the cool of the day **(Genesis 3:8)**, so did Enoch, demonstrating a restored communion after the fall.

Enoch's walk with God shows us that he was a man who recognized his sin, like Abel before him, and sought God's grace through sacrifice. Enoch pleased God because he understood the need for reconciliation, and he placed his trust in the Lord for his salvation. His faith was not a one-time act but a daily walk—a continuous fellowship with God over 300 years.

We also see this theme repeated in the lives of other faithful men of God. Noah, another figure who lived in a time of immense corruption, is described in **Genesis 6:9** as a man who *"**walked with God.**"* Despite the evil that surrounded him, Noah's faith was unwavering, and he too found favor with the Lord. God's call to walk with Him, to live blamelessly and righteously, echoed through the generations.

The patriarch Abraham, the father of faith, was also called to walk before God. **Genesis 17:1** records God's words to him: *"**I am the Almighty God; walk before me, and be thou perfect.**"* Despite his human failings, Abraham maintained a close relationship with God. As he neared the end of his life, Abraham's walk with God was still a defining aspect of his legacy, as he declared in **Genesis 24:40,** *"**The LORD, before whom I walk, will send his angel with thee, and prosper thy way.**"*

Walking with God, from Enoch to Noah to Abraham, is a picture of daily communion, step-by-step fellowship, and trust in God's faithfulness. It's a journey of reconciliation, where faith brings us into intimate fellowship with the Creator. As Jesus said in **John 10:27,** *"**My sheep hear my voice, and I know them, and they follow me.**"* This following, this walking with the Good Shepherd, continues to define the life of every believer today.

Jesus offers us the same opportunity for fellowship with

God that Enoch experienced. Through His sacrifice, Jesus reconciles us to God, encouraging us to walk in newness of life by being born again and renewing our minds. **Romans 6:4** reminds us, *"**Therefore we are buried with him by baptism into death: that like as Christ was raised up from the dead by the glory of the Father, even so we also should walk in newness of life."*** Like Enoch, Noah, and Abraham, we are called to walk in faith, trusting in God's promises and living in constant communion with Him.

As we reflect on the lives of these ancient men of faith, let us be encouraged to deepen our own walk with God. Let us seek daily fellowship with the Lord through Jesus Christ, who made it possible for us to be reconciled to the Father and to live a life that pleases Him. The invitation to walk with God is as real for us today as it was for Enoch, and the reward is eternal fellowship with the One who created and loves us.

---

# **Walk With God: A Journey of Faith and Eternal Promise**

---

Throughout Scripture, walking with God is a powerful expression of faith and intimacy with the Creator. **Hebrews 11:5-6** speaks of Enoch's extraordinary walk with God: *"**By faith Enoch was translated that he should not see death; and was not found, because God had translated him: for before his translation he had

**this testimony, that he pleased God. But without faith it is impossible to please him."*** Enoch's walk of faith was so pleasing to God that he escaped death, becoming a living illustration of salvation's ultimate promise—eternal life.

This idea of walking with God is not unique to Enoch. Adam and Eve, before the fall, walked with God in the cool of the day **(Genesis 3:8),** enjoying perfect fellowship. Later, in **Genesis 6:9**, Noah is described as a man who ***"walked with God."*** Despite the corruption of his time, Noah's faith set him apart, and he was spared from the judgment of the flood.

Abraham, too, was called to walk with God. In **Genesis 17:1**, God says to him, ***"I am the Almighty God; walk before me, and be thou perfect."*** Despite his human failings, Abraham's faith allowed him to walk closely with God, and through him, blessings flowed to all nations. **Genesis 24:40** records Abraham's confidence in God's guidance: ***"The LORD, before whom I walk, will send his angel with thee, and prosper thy way."*** Abraham's life, like Enoch's, was a step-by-step journey of fellowship with God.

## Jesus' Walk: The Ultimate Example of Faith

During His 3.5 years of ministry, Jesus Himself walked thousands of miles to fulfill His divine mission. Jesus traveled approximately 3,000 to 6,000 miles on foot, visiting regions from Galilee to Jerusalem, Judea, Samaria, and the Decapolis. His journeys, such as walking the 70-80 miles between Galilee and Jerusalem multiple times, demonstrated His dedication to teaching, healing, and proclaiming the kingdom of God. Jesus walked not only to cover physical ground but to model the spiritual journey we are all called to follow—a life lived by faith.

## Walking in Faith Leads to God's Promise

Just as Enoch walked with God and escaped death, and Noah and Abraham received their own blessings, we are called to live by faith. The example of these men illustrates that walking with God is not about perfection but about trust and obedience to God's will. **2 Corinthians 5:7** reminds us, *"For we walk by faith, not by sight."* Faith leads us to the ultimate promise— eternal life through Jesus Christ.

Enoch's life, in particular, illustrates the profound promise of salvation. He was not merely spared from death but taken directly into God's presence, a foreshadowing of the eternal reward awaiting those who walk with God. This echoes Jesus' words in **John 14:3, *"And if I go and prepare a place for you, I will come again, and receive you unto myself; that where I am, there ye may be also."***

# The Promise of Eternal Life

God chose Enoch to be a symbol of the resurrection and the life beyond this world. Job, another figure from the ancient world, also understood this promise, saying in

**Job 19:26,** *"**And though after my skin worms destroy this body, yet in my flesh shall I see God.**"* The early believers knew that life with God extended beyond the grave. Enoch's translation is the perfect illustration of this truth: that through faith, we too will be brought into the eternal presence of the Lord.

In **Genesis 5:24**, it is written, *"**And Enoch walked with God: and he was not; for God took him.**"* One moment Enoch was there, and then he was gone—no body, no trace. The Hebrew word for "took" implies a sudden, miraculous disappearance, and the explanation is clear: God took him because of his faith.

Enoch's story invites us to consider our own walk with God. Are we walking closely with Him, trusting in His promises, and living by faith as Enoch, Noah, Abraham, and Jesus did? The reward for such a walk is not just peace and blessings in this life but the promise of eternal life in God's presence. Through Jesus Christ, who walked this earth and conquered death, we have the hope of walking with God forever. As **John 10:27** says, *"**My sheep hear my voice, and I know them, and they follow me.**"*

Let Enoch's story inspire you to walk faithfully with God, trusting in His grace and looking forward to the ultimate reward—eternal life in His presence.

---

**\*\*Enoch – A Life of Faith and Divine Fellowship\*\***

---

Enoch's life is filled with remarkable details that set him apart in the biblical narrative. Here is a list of amazing facts about Enoch, supported by KJV scriptures, that highlight his unique walk with God and his role in biblical history:

### 1. **Enoch Lived a Life That Pleased God**
*"And Enoch walked with God: and he was not; for God took him."* (Genesis 5:24)

Enoch is one of the few people in the Bible described as walking with God. This phrase signifies a life of deep faith, intimacy, and obedience to the Lord.

### 2. **Enoch Did Not Experience Death**
*"By faith Enoch was translated that he should not see death; and was not found, because God had translated him: for before his translation he had this testimony, that he pleased God."* (Hebrews 11:5)

Enoch was miraculously taken directly to heaven without dying, which is an extremely rare occurrence in the Bible.

### 3. **Enoch Lived for 365 Years**
*"And all the days of Enoch were three hundred sixty and five years."* (Genesis 5:23)

Enoch lived for exactly 365 years, reflecting the days of a solar year. During this time, he maintained a close and faithful walk with God.

### 4. **Enoch Prophesied About the Second Coming of Christ**
*"And Enoch also, the seventh from Adam,

prophesied of these, saying, Behold, the Lord cometh with ten thousands of his saints."* (Jude 1:14)

Enoch is known for his prophecy concerning the Lord's return with His saints, a remarkable foresight thousands of years before Christ's earthly ministry.

### 5. **Enoch Was a Man of Great Faith**

*"But without faith it is impossible to please him: for he that cometh to God must believe that he is, and that he is a rewarder of them that diligently seek him."* (Hebrews 11:6)

Enoch's strong faith in God is the reason he pleased the Lord and was taken to heaven. His life exemplified the importance of unwavering belief and trust in God.

### 6. **Enoch Was the Seventh Generation from Adam**

*"And Enoch lived sixty and five years, and begat Methuselah."* (Genesis 5:21)

As the seventh generation from Adam, Enoch's place in the lineage of early humanity marks him as a significant figure in the unfolding of God's plan.

### 7. **Enoch's Prophetic Role Is Recognized in the New Testament**

*"To execute judgment upon all, and to convince all that are ungodly among them of all their ungodly deeds which they have ungodly committed, and of all their hard speeches which ungodly sinners have spoken against him."* (Jude 1:15)

Enoch's prophecy about God's coming judgment reveals his role as a voice of righteousness in a world that was increasingly corrupt.

## 8. **Enoch Walked with God for 300 Years After the Birth of His Son**

*"And Enoch walked with God after he begat Methuselah three hundred years, and begat sons and daughters."* (Genesis 5:22)

Enoch's close relationship with God continued for centuries, showing his long-lasting commitment to living a life of faith and fellowship with the Creator.

## 9. **Enoch's Life Is a Testament to the Rewards of Faith**

*"For before his translation he had this testimony, that he pleased God."* (Hebrews 11:5)

Enoch's life demonstrates that faithfulness to God brings great reward, as he was translated to heaven, bypassing death, as a result of his relationship with God.

## 10. **Enoch's Walk with God Is an Example for All Believers**

Enoch's unique story serves as an inspiration for believers to deepen their own fellowship with God and strive to live in unwavering faith. His life points to the ultimate reward of eternal life for those who walk with God, as Jesus said in **John 11:26, *"And whosoever liveth and believeth in me shall never die."***

Enoch's extraordinary walk with God continues to inspire generations of believers to pursue a life of faith, obedience, and close communion with the Lord. His legacy of faith, foretold in both the Old and New Testaments, reminds us of the promise of eternal life through Jesus Christ.

## DEVELOPING MUSCLES

During my high school years in 1972 when I was 14 years old, I had built a strong foundation in physical fitness, particularly through raccoon hunting, which strengthened my body in unexpected ways. One day in gym class, some of the boys were testing their strength with chin-ups and pull-ups. Now, pull-ups, done with an overhand grip, are especially challenging because they focus on the lats, shifting much of the effort away from the biceps.

By that time, I had been working out physically for several years, and my muscles were well developed from the tough work that came with raccoon hunting. Holding onto the dogs, walking miles through rough terrain—swamps, bogs, tall grass, and cornfields—while carrying one to three dead raccoons over my shoulder had conditioned my body.

At home, I had also taken up weightlifting, even though my brother had already gone off to the army. Despite weighing only 110 pounds, I had built enough strength to press 120 pounds over my head with my right hand and 90 pounds with my left, and I could press a total of 180 pounds over my head. These workouts gave me the confidence to test myself during that gym class.

So, I joined the boys and decided to see how many pull-ups I could do in one go. I started strong, and when I reached 20, the other boys began gathering around, watching with disbelief. Then I hit 30. Before long, I had completed over 40 pull-ups, setting a new record for the high school—one that lasted for many years.

## Outrunning Wisconsin's Cross Country Champion

In 1973, my family and I went up to our cabin at Yellow River. I brought along my friend David Koberson, who was my age and a well-known local cross-country champion. David had won his division in his grade, making him a formidable competitor in long-distance running.

One day, while we were out for a walk, I challenged David to a race. We took off, and to both of our surprise, I left him far behind, eventually winning the race by a large margin. We had probably run for over a mile, and even though David was a champion, my endurance won the day.

Looking back, I realized that the many hours spent raccoon hunting had given me a unique advantage. Running alongside the dogs, carrying raccoons, guns, and other equipment through difficult terrain had built up my stamina. It was the kind of unintentional training that prepared me for challenges like this, even against a trained champion.

These experiences taught me that strength and endurance are not just about formal training; sometimes, the hard work and persistence found in everyday tasks build us up for challenges we don't expect.

**"But they that wait upon the Lord shall renew their strength; they shall mount up with wings as eagles; they shall run, and not be weary; and they shall walk, and not faint"\* (Isaiah 40:31, KJV).** This verse reminds me that God equips us in unexpected ways, preparing us for the races we don't even know we're training for.

# CHAPTER THREE
## ** Walking with God: A Journey of Faith and Intimate Communion**

---

In **Hebrews 11:5-6**, we find a powerful example of what it means to walk with God through the life of Enoch. The scripture tells us, *"**By faith Enoch was translated that he should not see death; and was not found, because God had translated him: for before his translation he had this testimony, that he pleased God. But without faith it is impossible to please him.**"* Enoch's life is a reminder that walking with God is not just about obedience, but about faith, trust, and a personal relationship with the Creator.

From the beginning, God has always desired intimate fellowship with humanity. Adam and Eve walked with God in the Garden of Eden **(Genesis 3:8),** but sin broke that perfect communion. Yet through Enoch, the true destiny of man—restoration and communion with God—is revealed once again. Enoch's life shows that God is not distant, but a personal and present God who desires fellowship with His people. He entered into this relationship through faith, recognizing the need for sacrifice, repentance, and submission to God's will.

In the same way that Abel recognized the need for a sacrifice for sin, which pointed to Christ's future death, Enoch must have also understood the concept of sacrifice, repentance, and faith. Enoch's walk with God is a timeless illustration of faith, a life lived in step with God that one day culminates in eternal glory.

### The Lesson of Faith: Walking with God

**Hebrews 11:6** emphasizes the core lesson of Enoch's life: *"**Without faith, it is impossible to please Him.**"* Walking with God, pleasing God, and ultimately entering into His eternal presence is impossible without faith. This is a foundational truth of the Christian life—faith is the only way to be reconciled with God.

No amount of religious works, ceremonies, or external rituals can bring us into that intimate relationship with God. **Romans 3:20** reminds us, *"**Therefore by the deeds of the law there shall no flesh be justified in his sight.**"* True reconciliation with God is through faith alone. Enoch's life demonstrates this reality, as does the life of Abel, who by faith offered an acceptable sacrifice to God.

### Faith, that gives birth to Works, Pleases God

In **Hebrews 11**, Enoch is highlighted as an example of what it means to live by faith. This echoes the message found throughout the Bible: *"**For by grace are ye saved through faith; and that not of yourselves: it is the gift of God: Not of works, lest any man should boast.**"* **(Ephesians 2:8-9)**. Faith is the key that unlocks the door to pleasing God and walking in His presence. **Galatians 5:6** further clarifies, *"**For in Jesus Christ neither circumcision availeth any thing, nor uncircumcision; but faith which worketh by love.**"*

Faith, then, is not merely intellectual belief; it is active, alive, and expressed through love. Enoch's faith was dynamic, and it led him to walk closely with God for 300 years. His life was a testimony to the kind of faith that pleases God—faith that trusts in Him, seeks Him daily, and lives in step with His will.

## The Walk of Faith Leads to Eternal Life

Enoch's translation into heaven without experiencing death serves as a powerful symbol of the reward of faith. His life, like that of Noah and Abraham, reveals the eternal promise that awaits those who walk with God. Jesus Himself spoke of this promise in **John 11:25-26**, saying, *"**I am the resurrection, and the life: he that believeth in me, though he were dead, yet shall he live: And whosoever liveth and believeth in me shall never die.**"*

Enoch's life points us to the ultimate truth that walking with God is not just for this life, but for eternity. Just as Enoch was taken to be with God, those who place their faith in Jesus Christ will one day be with Him in eternal glory. This promise is the foundation of the Christian faith, and Enoch's life serves as a timeless example of what it means to live in intimate communion with God.

As we reflect on Enoch's story, we are reminded that walking with God is a daily, step-by-step journey of faith. It is a journey that requires trust, repentance, and the recognition of our need for God's grace. Like Enoch, we are called to walk closely with God, and through faith in Jesus Christ, we can experience the same promise of eternal life in His presence.

## **Faith that Pleases God: Enoch's Journey of Trust and Obedience**

---

From the beginning, faith has been the foundation of a life that pleases God. Abel believed and obeyed the command of God by offering the proper sacrifice, demonstrating his faith. **Hebrews 11:4** says, *"By faith Abel offered unto God a more excellent sacrifice than Cain."* Enoch, the next example in Hebrews 11, continued this walk of faith, trusting God as his Savior and living in such a way that he was reconciled to God and ultimately taken up into heaven without experiencing death.

In humanity's fallen state, nothing done in the flesh can please God. **Romans 8:8** reminds us, *"So then they that are in the flesh cannot please God."* It is faith alone that pleases Him. Enoch exemplified this faith, as **Hebrews 11:5** states, *****"By faith Enoch was translated that he should not see death; and was not found, because God had translated him."*** His trust in God allowed him to walk with the Lord in close fellowship, leading to his divine translation into heaven.

## What Does It Mean to Have Faith in God?

The essence of faith begins with believing that God is who He says He is. **Hebrews 11:6** states, *****"But without faith it is impossible to please him: for he that cometh to God must believe that he is, and that he is a rewarder of them that diligently seek him."*** This belief is not a vague or general acknowledgment of a higher power, but a trust in the true God as revealed in His Word.

Faith in God requires believing not just in any god or concept of divinity, but in the one true God who has revealed Himself throughout history. In the early days of human existence, God made Himself known to people like Enoch, who believed in this revealed God and walked in obedience to Him.

For us, that revelation is even clearer. We are called to believe in the God of Abraham, Isaac, and Jacob, the God who became incarnate in Jesus Christ. **John 14:6** makes it clear that salvation is only possible through Jesus when He said, *****"I am the way, the truth, and the life: no man cometh unto the Father, but by me."*** To have faith that pleases God, one must believe in the fullness of who God is, including the revelation of His Son, Jesus

Christ.

## The True Revelation of God

It is not enough to have a general belief in God; we must believe in the God who has revealed Himself fully. The God of the Old Testament is also the God and Father of our Lord Jesus Christ, as made known in the New Testament. This Trinitarian understanding of God—Father, the Word, and Holy Spirit—shows us the complete nature of God's being.

Some might argue that belief in the Old Testament revelation of God is enough, but the New Testament reveals the fullness of God's nature through Jesus Christ. **Hebrews 1:1-2** says, ***"God, who at sundry times and in divers manners spake in time past unto the fathers by the prophets, hath in these last days spoken unto us by his Son."*** To know God, we must accept His complete revelation, which includes His manifestation in Jesus Christ.

## Faith in Jesus Christ: The Fulfillment of God's Revelation

Enoch's walk with God teaches us that faith requires a deep trust in who God truly is. Today, that faith is centered on Jesus Christ. **1 John 5:11-12** says, ***"And this is the record, that God hath given to us eternal life, and this life is in his Son. He that hath the Son hath life; and he that hath not the Son of God hath***

**not life."*** Just as Enoch trusted in the revelation he received and was rewarded with eternal life, we too must trust in the full revelation of God through Jesus Christ to receive eternal life.

Faith that pleases God involves understanding that Jesus is the fulfillment of all the promises made in the Old Testament. **Acts 4:12** confirms this, saying, ***"Neither is there salvation in any other: for there is none other name under heaven given among men, whereby we must be saved."*** Through faith in Jesus, we experience reconciliation with God and the promise of eternal life, just as Enoch did when he was taken up to be with God.

In conclusion, Enoch's story reminds us that to walk with God and please Him, we must have faith in the true and living God. Today, that faith is expressed through trust in Jesus Christ, who reveals the fullness of God's nature and offers us the gift of eternal life. **As Hebrews 11:6** says, ***"For he that cometh to God must believe that he is, and that he is a rewarder of them that diligently seek him."*** Faith in Jesus, the Son of God, is the ultimate key to walking with God and receiving His eternal reward.

---

## **Enoch: A Journey of Faith in the True God**

---

Enoch's testimony of faith and reconciliation with God began with his belief in the true God, the God who revealed Himself as holy, righteous, and the judge of sin. **Genesis 5:24** says, *"**And Enoch walked with God: and he was not; for God took him.**"* This simple yet profound statement highlights Enoch's deep relationship with God, one built on trust and faith in who God truly is.

Enoch believed in the God who required a sacrifice for sin, the God who made it clear that no man could earn his way to heaven through works. Enoch's faith was grounded in the understanding that God is holy and just, and that a sacrifice was needed to cover sin—a truth that would later be fully revealed through the sacrifice of Jesus Christ.

In today's world, there is a tendency to reduce faith to a mere belief in a higher power or a monotheistic concept of God. But as Enoch's life shows us, believing in God means accepting the full revelation of who He is. This is especially important for us today because that revelation now includes Jesus Christ, the Son of God. Jesus Himself said in **John 14:6,** *"**I am the way, the truth, and the life: no man cometh unto the Father, but by me.**"* Faith in God is incomplete without faith in His Son, Jesus Christ.

## Knowing God as He Truly Is

In **Acts 17,** Paul addresses the people of Athens who worshipped many gods, including an altar inscribed to an **"unknown god."** Paul explained to them that the true God is the Creator of all things, saying, *"**God that made the world and all things therein, seeing that he is Lord of heaven and earth.**"* **(Acts 17:24).** Enoch would have known this, too—he understood that God was the Creator and Sustainer of everything. Enoch knew that God was righteous, the source of all morality, and a God of judgment.

But Enoch's understanding of God didn't stop at knowing Him as Creator. He also knew that God was a God of mercy and salvation. Enoch's prophecy, seen through the naming of his son Methuselah (which means "his death will bring judgment"), reflects his awareness of God's coming judgment and the need for repentance.

Paul continued in **Acts 17,** explaining that while God had overlooked times of ignorance in the past, He now calls all men to repent because He has appointed a day to judge the world in righteousness through Jesus Christ, whom He raised from the dead. This is the fullness of God's revelation, and it is this complete understanding of God that saves. **Romans 10:9** says, *****"That if thou shalt confess with thy mouth the Lord Jesus, and shalt believe in thine heart that God hath raised him from the dead, thou shalt be saved."*****

## Enoch's Faith: Trusting in God's Promise

Enoch's faith didn't just stop at knowing God; he trusted in God's promise to reward those who seek Him. **Hebrews 11:6** tells us, *****"But without faith it is impossible to please him: for he that cometh to God must believe that he is, and that he is a rewarder of them that diligently seek him."***** Enoch believed that God was not only the Creator and Judge but also the Redeemer. He trusted that God would save those who earnestly sought Him, and this trust was at the core of his faith.

The same principle applies to us today. God still rewards those who diligently seek Him, but this reward comes through faith in Jesus Christ. **Hebrews 1:1-2** says, ***"God, who at sundry times and in divers manners spake in time past unto the fathers by the prophets, Hath in these last days spoken unto us by his Son."*** Jesus is the completion of God's revelation, and our faith in Him is what reconciles us to God, just as Enoch's faith reconciled him to the Creator.

## Conclusion: Walking by Faith, Following Christ

Enoch's life serves as a powerful example of what it means to walk by faith. He believed in the true God and trusted in His promise of redemption. His faith was not vague or incomplete, but grounded in the full revelation of God as both Judge and Redeemer. For us today, this means believing in Jesus Christ as the fulfillment of God's promise. Enoch's walk with God is a testimony to the fact that faith in the true God is the key to eternal life.

As we consider Enoch's journey, let us be reminded that faith in God means believing in the fullness of His revelation, including the salvation offered through Jesus Christ. Just as Enoch walked with God and was taken up into His presence, so too are we called to walk by faith in Jesus and one day enter into the eternal reward God has prepared for those who love Him.

# **Enoch's Walk of Faith: Seeking the God Who Rewards**

---

Enoch believed in a personal, loving, and forgiving God—a God who rewards those who earnestly seek Him. **Hebrews 11:6** reminds us, ***"But without faith it is impossible to please him: for he that cometh to God must believe that he is, and that he is a rewarder of them that diligently seek him."*** This faith defined Enoch's life. Unlike some distant, impersonal force, Enoch knew the true God—a God who desires fellowship, offers salvation, and welcomes those who seek Him with a repentant heart.

Throughout Scripture, God's promise to reward those who seek Him is clear. David, in **1 Chronicles 28:9**, gave this counsel to his son Solomon: ***"If thou seek him, he will be found of thee."*** David himself reflected this truth in **Psalm 119:10:** ***"With my whole heart have I sought thee."*** Likewise, in **Proverbs 8:17**, God assures us, ***"I love them that love me; and those that seek me early shall find me."*** This is the essence of the God Enoch walked with—a God who is eager to be found by those who seek Him.

# A God Who Saves and Rewards

Unlike other religions where deities are often viewed as distant or punishing, the God of the Bible is a rewarder of those who seek Him in faith. **Psalm 58:11** declares, *"Verily there is a reward for the righteous."* This reward is not based on human merit but on God's grace and the heart of the seeker. **Proverbs 11:18** echoes this truth: *"To him that soweth righteousness shall be a sure reward."*

God's ultimate expression of being a rewarder is seen in His gift of salvation through Jesus Christ. **John 3:16** proclaims, *"For God so loved the world, that he gave his only begotten Son, that whosoever believeth in him should not perish, but have everlasting life."* Through faith in Christ, the greatest reward is given—eternal life. Jesus further promises in **John 6:37**, *"Him that cometh to me I will in no wise cast out."*

God is not only a Savior by nature but a generous rewarder. When we seek Him, we are promised an abundance of blessings. As Jesus said in **Matthew 6:33**, *"But seek ye first the kingdom of God, and his righteousness; and all these things shall be added unto you."* God's blessings are not just material but spiritual and eternal. **Ephesians 1:3** confirms, *"Blessed be the God and Father of our Lord Jesus Christ, who hath blessed us with all spiritual blessings in heavenly places in Christ."*

# Jesus: The Way to the Father

Enoch's faith teaches us that seeking God must be done on His terms, and today, that means seeking Him through Jesus Christ. Jesus declared in **John 14:6**, *"I am the

**way, the truth, and the life: no man cometh unto the Father, but by me."*** Salvation is found only in Christ, as **Acts 4:12** tells us, ***"Neither is there salvation in any other: for there is none other name under heaven given among men, whereby we must be saved."***

God's desire is to lavishly reward those who come to Him in faith through His Son. He grants forgiveness, peace, a new heart, and eternal life. Enoch's walk with God points us to the same truth: God is a Savior who seeks to reward those who come to Him with faith and humility.

Enoch's life is a testimony that the walk of faith begins with knowing God as He truly is—a personal, loving God who rewards those who diligently seek Him through faith in Jesus Christ.

# **Enoch: A Prophet of Faith in a Time of Apostasy**

---

Enoch, as recorded in Scripture, stands out as the first prophet whose words are remembered in a time of growing apostasy. He is particularly noted for the prophecy he delivered regarding the coming judgment, a revelation that led him to name his son Methuselah, whose name means, ***"When he dies, judgment shall be sent."*** **(Genesis 5:21-24).** Methuselah, who lived the longest in biblical history, exemplifies God's grace, as his life delayed the judgment, giving humanity ample time to repent. Some rabbinical sources even claim that Methuselah died one week before the flood, just as Noah entered the Ark. What we do know from Scripture is that Methuselah died in the year of the flood, showcasing both the urgency and patience of God's judgment.

Enoch's prophetic message and life were in direct confrontation with the apostates of his time. **Jude 1:14-15** refers to Enoch's prophecy, warning of judgment upon the ungodly. Apostasy, characterized by murmuring, complaining, and following after lusts, was rampant in Enoch's day—echoes of which are seen in Israel's rebellion, the angels' disobedience, and the sins of Sodom and Gomorrah.

# Enoch's Walk of Faith

**Hebrews 11:5** declares, ***"By faith Enoch was translated that he should not see death; and was not found, because God had translated him: for before his translation he had this testimony, that he pleased God."*** Enoch's faith is central to his pleasing walk with God. It wasn't just his works that pleased God, but his trust in who God is. Twice in **Genesis 5:22-24**, the Scriptures emphasize that Enoch *"walked with God."* His walk was a testimony to a life lived in harmony and fellowship with the Creator, even amidst a corrupt and decaying world.

The Bible notes that Enoch lived in a time of unparalleled corruption. Despite this, Enoch's life was marked by faithfulness and a close relationship with God. His walk with God assumed reconciliation, for two cannot walk together unless they are agreed, as **Amos 3:3** reminds us. Enoch's walk was a journey of agreement with God, one that assumed salvation and the restoration of fellowship with the Lord.

# A Life Pleasing to God

Enoch lived in a time not unlike ours—where the wickedness of society was prevalent, and the righteous were few. In fact, Jesus compared the days of Noah, and by extension, the days of Enoch, to the time just before His second coming. In **Matthew 24:37-38**, Jesus said, *"**But as the days of Noah were, so shall also the coming of the Son of man be.**"* The corruption of Enoch's day echoes the spiritual and moral decay we witness today, yet Enoch's life serves as a powerful example of how to walk faithfully with God amidst a sinful world.

Enoch's life spanned 365 years—years filled with both the joys of family and the challenges of a decaying society. Imagine Enoch, as a father, raising children in such a world, sharing with Mrs. Enoch concerns about their survival in such wicked times. It wasn't easy, just as it isn't easy today, but Enoch's solution was to walk with God, to remain in close fellowship, trusting in His plan and providence.

# The Elements of Enoch's Walk

Enoch's walk with God contains vital components for understanding what it means to live a life that pleases God:

## 1. **Reconciliation with God**:

Walking with God assumes reconciliation. **Romans 5:10** reminds us, ***"For if, when we were enemies, we were reconciled to God by the death of his Son, much more, being reconciled, we shall be saved by his life."*** Enoch's walk with God was possible because he had been reconciled to Him. This reconciliation was not the result of Enoch's own works, but of God's grace.

## 2. **Faith in God's Nature**:

Enoch believed in the true nature of God, knowing that He is personal, gracious, and forgiving. Hebrews 11:6 states, ***"But without faith it is impossible to please him: for he that cometh to God must believe that he is, and that he is a rewarder of them that diligently seek him."*** Enoch trusted that God was not just a distant force, but a personal Savior who rewards those who seek Him with faith and repentance.

## 3. **Walking in Agreement**:

As **Amos 3:3** says, ***"Can two walk together, except they be agreed?"*** Enoch's life reflected a walk in harmony with God's will. Enoch wasn't conformed to the corrupt ways of the world; instead, he walked according to God's truth, living in agreement with God's commandments and expectations. His life was a testimony of faith, obedience, and reliance on God's grace.

4. **An Example of Faith in Action**:
Enoch's walk with God was not passive; it was an active, daily journey of faith. **James 2:26** tells us, *"For as the body without the spirit is dead, so faith without works is dead also."* Enoch's faith produced fruit in his life, demonstrating what it means to walk in faith and trust in God.

# Conclusion: Walking with God in a World of Apostasy

Enoch's life is a testimony to the power of walking with God, even in times of great apostasy. His faith and reconciliation with God were central to his walk, and they serve as a model for believers today. Enoch's life shows us that even when surrounded by corruption, it is possible to live a life that pleases God, one that is marked by faith, trust, and daily fellowship with the Creator.

Enoch's story also foreshadows the ultimate walk of faith—our walk with Jesus Christ. **John 14:6** reminds us, *"I am the way, the truth, and the life: no man cometh unto the Father, but by me."* Through Christ, we are reconciled to God, able to walk with Him in faith, and assured of the reward of eternal life. As we look to Enoch's example, we are encouraged to continue our walk of faith, knowing that God is faithful and will reward those who seek Him diligently.

# The Beginning of My Spiritual Walk

The journey to freedom begins when we take hold of God's grace by faith. It is faith that brings victory over the world, as the Bible says, *"For whatsoever is born of God overcometh the world: and this is the victory that overcometh the world, even our faith"* (1 John 5:4, KJV). The sins we must overcome through grace by faith are clearly outlined in Galatians 5 and echoed throughout scripture.

Before I was born again, my life was consumed by addictions—pornography, drugs, alcohol, smoking tobacco, smokeless tobacco, violence, and ungodly music. My favorites were marijuana, vodka, Southern Comfort, Ripple wine, and Pabst Blue Ribbon beer. The music that filled my soul was from bands like Dr. Hook and the Medicine Show, the Grateful Dead, Pink Floyd, and America. I was entrenched in this lifestyle and had tried many times, in my own strength, to quit. But every effort ended in discouragement and failure.

I had reached such a point of despair that I decided to end my life. I was in the act of preparing to slit my wrists when the fear of God suddenly overwhelmed me. Dropping to my knees, I cried out to Jesus. In that very moment, He came gloriously into my life. It was as if faith in Christ immediately activated God's grace, and I was set free from every chain that had bound me. I'm telling you, Jesus set me free! And from that day forward, I've never boasted about my own ability to overcome.

For nearly 50 years, I've given all the glory to Christ.

Have I reached perfection? No. But do I still engage in the things I once did? Absolutely not. Have I stumbled along the way? Yes, I have. But each time, I repent and get back up. By God's true grace, through faith, and by hiding His Word in my heart, I am given victory over the world, the flesh, and the devil. As it is written, *"**Thy word have I hid in mine heart, that I might not sin against thee" (Psalm 119:11, KJV).***

I thank Jesus every day for the strength to stand, not by my own power, but by His. The truth is clear: *"**For by grace are ye saved through faith; and that not of yourselves: it is the gift of God: Not of works, lest any man should boast"* (Ephesians 2:8-9, KJV).** Every victory, every deliverance, belongs to Him.

Even the scripture warns us of those who would turn God's grace into a license for sin. As **Jude 1:4** says, *"**For there are certain men crept in unawares, who were before of old ordained to this condemnation, ungodly men, turning the grace of our God into lasciviousness, and denying the only Lord God, and our Lord Jesus Christ."*** We must be vigilant, holding fast to the true grace of God, which brings us into righteousness and freedom.

Thank you, Jesus, for the ongoing victory through Your grace.

# CHAPTER FOUR
## **Walking with God: The Journey of Faith and Transformation**

---

Walking with God is more than just a metaphor for living a godly life—it is a deep, spiritual reality that Enoch exemplified. When the Bible says that Enoch *"walked with God"* (Genesis 5:24), it speaks to the profound transformation and reconciliation that allowed him to have fellowship with the Creator. Walking with God requires a corresponding nature, reconciliation, and moral fitness, all of which come through the transforming power of salvation in Jesus Christ.

# Reconciliation with God

The first step to walking with God is reconciliation. As **Amos 3:3** asks, *"Can two walk together, except they be agreed?"* To walk with God, there must first be agreement, and that agreement can only come through being reconciled to God. **Romans 5:10 tells us, *"For if, when we were enemies, we were reconciled to God by the death of his Son, much more, being reconciled, we shall be saved by his life."*** Enoch, like every believer, was once an enemy of God, but through faith, he was reconciled and brought into agreement with God's will.

When we walk with God, we no longer live for ourselves. **Ephesians 4:22-24** teaches that the old self is put off, and the new self is created in righteousness and holiness. Enoch's life stands as a testimony to this transformation. He lived in a time of deep corruption, yet his faith in God allowed him to walk in agreement with the Lord, setting him apart from the world around him.

**A Corresponding Nature: Becoming a New Creation**

To walk with God, there must also be a corresponding nature—a shared spiritual connection that allows fellowship. **2 Corinthians 5:17 says, *"Therefore if any man be in Christ, he is a new creature: old things are passed away; behold, all things are become new."*** Without being born again, without sharing in God's divine nature, it is impossible to walk with Him.

In our sinful nature, we are separated from God. As **2 Corinthians 6:14** reminds us, ***"What fellowship hath righteousness with unrighteousness? and what communion hath light with darkness?"*** The gap between God and a sinner is vast, like the gap between a human and an animal—there is no shared nature, no common ground for true fellowship. But when we are saved, we are given a new nature, one that corresponds to God's righteousness. This is what enables us to walk with Him in fellowship and communion.

## Moral Fitness: Living a Life that Pleases God

Walking with God also presupposes moral fitness. God is holy and righteous, and He does not walk in fellowship with those who continue in sin. **1 Peter 1:16** commands us, *"**Be ye holy; for I am holy.**"* This holiness is not something we achieve on our own—it is a result of God's transformative work in us through salvation.

**2 Corinthians 6:14-16** emphasizes the necessity of living in righteousness to walk with God: *"**What fellowship hath righteousness with unrighteousness? ... For ye are the temple of the living God; as God hath said, I will dwell in them, and walk in them; and I will be their God, and they shall be my people.**"* God walks with those who have been morally transformed by His grace, those who are committed to living a life that reflects His holiness.

Enoch, through his faith, demonstrated this moral fitness. **Hebrews 11:5-6** tells us, *"**By faith Enoch was translated that he should not see death; and was not found, because God had translated him: for before his translation he had this testimony, that he pleased God.**"* His walk with God was marked by obedience, righteousness, and faith—qualities that allowed him to experience the unique privilege of being taken into heaven without experiencing death.

# The Walk of Faith in Jesus Christ

In the same way that Enoch walked with God through faith, we too are called to walk in faith, trusting in Jesus Christ as our Savior. **John 14:6** reminds us, ***"I am the way, the truth, and the life: no man cometh unto the Father, but by me."*** Just as Enoch trusted in the God who would one day send the Messiah, we trust in the completed work of Jesus Christ, who has reconciled us to God and made it possible for us to walk with Him.

Jesus is the perfect example of walking in harmony with God. He lived a life fully pleasing to the Father, demonstrating the perfect walk of faith, obedience, and love. Through Him, we are given the righteousness required to walk with God, not by our own merit, but through the grace and salvation offered by Christ.

### Conclusion: Walking in Agreement with God

Enoch's walk with God is an example for all believers today. It reminds us that walking with God is not a casual stroll; it requires reconciliation, transformation, and moral fitness. Through faith in Jesus Christ, we are reconciled to God, given a new nature, and empowered to live a life that pleases Him.

As we walk with God, we experience the joy of fellowship with the Creator, the assurance of His guidance, and the promise of eternal life. Like Enoch, may we walk in faith, trusting in God's grace and righteousness, as we journey through this life and into the next.

# **Walking with God: A Life of Holiness and Fellowship**

---

Walking with God is more than just a spiritual metaphor; it is an active, intentional journey of faith, righteousness, and communion with Him. Enoch's life, as described in **Genesis 5:24, *"And Enoch walked with God: and he was not; for God took him,"*** provides a powerful example of what it means to live in constant fellowship with the Creator. But walking with God is not something that happens by chance—it requires holiness, a desire for fellowship, and a commitment to live according to God's righteousness.

# The Path of Holiness

God never deviates from the path of holiness. **1 John 1:5** reminds us, ***"God is light, and in him is no darkness at all."*** He cannot and does not tolerate sin or unrighteousness. If we are to walk with God, we must also walk in holiness. This is why before God would dwell among the people of Israel, all that was defiled had to be removed from the camp **(Numbers 5:2)**. Similarly, before the millennial kingdom begins, all that offends must be cleansed from the earth **(Matthew 13:41)**.

To walk with God, we must first be made righteous in His sight. This righteousness is not something we earn on our own, but something that is imputed to us through faith, as the New Testament reveals in **Romans 4:22-24**. However, this concept of imputed righteousness is also present in the Old Testament. Enoch, Noah, and Abraham walked with God, and this was only possible because they were covered by God's righteousness. God demands holiness from all who seek fellowship with Him, and through the righteousness given to us by Christ, we are able to meet that standard.

# The Desire for Fellowship

Walking with God also implies a deep desire for fellowship with Him. **Psalm 42:1** expresses this longing: *"**As the hart panteth after the water brooks, so panteth my soul after thee, O God.**"* It is not enough to merely claim faith; there must be a yearning to walk in close communion with God. Enoch walked with God for 300 years **(Genesis 5:22),** demonstrating a sustained, intentional pursuit of fellowship with the Lord.

This desire for fellowship extends to being in the presence of fellow believers. **Hebrews 10:25** urges us, *"**Not forsaking the assembling of ourselves together, as the manner of some is; but exhorting one another: and so much the more, as ye see the day approaching.**"* Just as being in fellowship with God brings us joy and strength, being in fellowship with other believers helps us grow in love and good works. This community of faith strengthens our walk with God, keeping us accountable and encouraging us in our pursuit of holiness.

# Walking in the Spirit

Enoch's walk with God was intentional, not accidental. Pleasing God is not something that happens automatically—it is something we must pursue with passion and discipline. **Galatians 5:16** commands us to *"**walk in the Spirit, and ye shall not fulfil the lust of the flesh."*** Walking with God means being led by the Spirit, allowing His guidance to direct every step of our journey.

## The New Testament provides us with several key principles for walking with God:

- **Walk in Truth**: 3 John 1:4 says, *"**I have no greater joy than to hear that my children walk in truth."*** Walking with God requires living according to His truth, as revealed in His Word.

- **Walk in Honesty**: Romans 13:13 calls us to walk *"**honestly, as in the day; not in rioting and drunkenness, not in chambering and wantonness, not in strife and envying."*** Honesty and integrity are vital components of walking with God.

- **Walk in Love**: Ephesians 5:2 instructs us to *"walk in love, as Christ also hath loved us."* Love is central to the Christian walk, reflecting the character of God in our interactions with others.
- **Walk in Light**: Ephesians 5:8 calls us to walk *"as children of light."* When we walk in the light, we reject the works of darkness and live in the truth of God's holiness.

- **Walk in Wisdom**: Ephesians 5:15 urges us to *"walk circumspectly, not as fools, but as wise."* Wisdom comes from fearing the Lord and following His commands.

- **Walk in Holiness**: Ephesians 2:10 reminds us that *"we are his workmanship, created in Christ Jesus unto good works."* We are called to walk in the holiness that God has given us through Christ.

# Conclusion: A Life Pleasing to God

Enoch's life teaches us that walking with God is not something passive or accidental—it is intentional, disciplined, and driven by a desire for holiness and fellowship with Him. As **Hebrews 11:5** says, *"For before his translation he had this testimony, that he pleased God."* Pleasing God requires living in harmony with His will, walking in the Spirit, and committing ourselves to a life of righteousness.

In the New Testament, the call to walk with God is further illuminated by the life and teachings of Jesus

Christ. Through Him, we are reconciled to God, given His righteousness, and empowered to walk in holiness. Let us, like Enoch, choose to walk with God each day, trusting in His grace and pursuing a life that is pleasing to Him.

# **Enoch: The Man Who Walked With God**

---

Enoch stands out in biblical history as a man who not only walked with God but was taken up to heaven without seeing death. His life of faith and unwavering dedication offers profound lessons for every believer. Enoch lived in a time of growing corruption, yet he stood as a beacon of righteousness, a man who pleased God and served as a preacher of judgment against ungodliness.

**Key Lessons from Enoch's Life:**

1. **Walking with God Requires Faith and Righteousness**

Hebrews 11:5-6 states, *"By faith Enoch was translated that he should not see death; and was not found, because God had translated him: for before his translation he had this testimony, that he pleased

**God. But without faith it is impossible to please him."*** Enoch's life exemplifies that pleasing God comes from a heart rooted in faith, walking step by step in His righteousness.

## 2. **Holiness Is Non-Negotiable in Walking with God**

Walking with God implies holiness. In **1 John 1:5**, we are reminded that ***"God is light, and in him is no darkness at all."*** To walk with God, we must embrace holiness, for He will not dwell with uncleanliness. Enoch lived this reality, being reconciled to God through faith and walking in righteousness for 300 years **(Genesis 5:22)**.

## 3. **A Desire for Fellowship with God Must Drive Our Walk**

Enoch's life challenges us to yearn for fellowship with God. He was not content with mere belief but pursued a life of intimate communion with his Creator. Psalm 42:1 declares, ***"As the hart panteth after the water brooks, so panteth my soul after thee, O God."*** True believers seek God not just out of duty but out of a deep, heartfelt desire to be in His presence.

## 4. **Walking with God Involves Speaking His Truth Boldly**

Enoch's walk with God extended beyond personal holiness. As a preacher, he boldly proclaimed the coming judgment of God. **Jude 1:14-15** records his prophecy: *"Behold, the Lord cometh with ten thousands of his saints, to execute judgment upon all."* Enoch did not shy away from confronting the false teachers and the ungodliness around him. His message of judgment was a reflection of his walk with God in a corrupt world.

5. **The Prophecy of Final Judgment**

Enoch's prophecy in Jude is not just about the flood in Noah's day, but about the final judgment when the Lord will return with His saints to judge the world. His message speaks to the ultimate fulfillment of God's justice. As believers, we are called to live with this eternal perspective, knowing that the righteous Judge will come.

---

# Conclusion: Walking in the Spirit

Enoch's life serves as a model for us today. To walk with God is to live in holiness, seek constant fellowship with Him, and boldly proclaim His truth in a world that often rejects it. As Galatians 5:16 reminds us, *"Walk in the Spirit, and ye shall not fulfil the lust of the flesh."* Like Enoch, we are called to walk in faith, truth, love, and righteousness, knowing that our walk with God will ultimately lead us to eternal life in His presence.

Enoch's life foreshadows the ultimate fellowship we will have with God through Christ Jesus.

## **"Walking with God: A Journey Like Enoch's, a Call to Divine Fellowship"**

The return of Christ with many thousands of His angels is a prophecy that has been foretold, pointing to the culmination of human history. This truth, as we see in the Scriptures, parallels the message of Enoch. He preached the coming judgment long before the flood and far before the final judgment, which is yet to come. Although he never witnessed these events firsthand, his unwavering faith in God's promises is a profound example of how a believer lives with the certainty of God's word.

In a way, Enoch's life is similar to that of a New Testament believer. While we anticipate the final judgment, believers in Christ have the hope of being caught up in the rapture before God's judgment is poured out upon the earth. Enoch, in his time, serves as an illustration of this pre-tribulation rapture, a foreshadowing of what believers will experience just before the final moments of this world. As **1 Thessalonians 4:16-17** tells us, **"For the Lord himself shall descend from heaven with a shout, with the voice of the archangel, and with the trump of God: and the dead in Christ shall rise first: Then we which are alive and remain shall be caught up together with them in the clouds, to meet the Lord in the air: and so shall we ever be with the Lord" (KJV).**

Imagine the moment when millions of believers, like

Enoch, will be taken up to meet the Lord. In a twinkling of an eye, as Paul describes in **1 Corinthians 15:52,** the faithful will disappear from the face of the earth. Then, as Enoch's story foreshadows, judgment will descend. His life, therefore, not only represents the promise of heaven but also the assurance of deliverance from God's wrath for those who walk with Him in faith.

But more than this prophecy, Enoch's life is an enduring example of what it means to truly walk with God. In **Genesis 5:24**, it is written, **"And Enoch walked with God: and he was not; for God took him" (KJV).** His intimate relationship with the Creator serves as a model for us all. The essence of his story is not just about his escape from judgment, but about the depth of his communion with God—a walk so evident that it was his defining trait.

In this reflection, let us take the example of Enoch and strive to walk with God daily, knowing that one day we too shall be caught up to meet the Lord in glory

## How the Four Gospels Transformed My Life

On February 18, 1975, my life was forever changed when I gave my heart to Jesus Christ. At that moment, all I had was a small, military-green Bible. As soon as Christ entered my heart, I picked up that little Bible and began devouring it. The four Gospels—Matthew, Mark, Luke, and John—became my favorite books. I couldn't get enough of the powerful reality of Jesus. Through those pages, I walked with Christ from His birth to His childhood, through His baptism by John, and into the wilderness, where He boldly overcame the enemy by declaring, *"It is written."*

For the first three years of my faith journey, I focused almost entirely on Jesus as revealed in the four Gospels. While I read the epistles and appreciated them, nothing captured my heart like the life, words, and ministry of Christ. I was captivated by His teachings and in awe of His perfect reflection of the Father's love.

I wept when I read about His sufferings, crucifixion, and death. The moment when the Heavenly Father had to turn His face away from His own Son pierced my heart, because I knew He did it out of love for us. And I rejoiced in His victory over every satanic power, celebrating the triumphant conquest He won on our behalf. One of my favorite passages outside the Gospels is from Hebrews:

*"God, who at sundry times and in divers manners spake in time past unto the fathers by the prophets, Hath in these last days spoken unto us by his Son, whom he hath appointed heir of all things, by whom also he made the worlds; Who being the brightness of his glory, and the express image of his person, and upholding all things by the word of his power, when he had by himself purged our sins, sat down on the right hand of the Majesty on high"* (Hebrews 1:1-3, KJV).

Jesus Christ is the perfect reflection of the Heavenly Father. There is no greater revelation of God's will than the life of Jesus. Looking back, I am thankful that I was not influenced by much of the modern-day church during the first three years of my salvation. After living and ministering in Alaska for almost five years, I came to the lower 48 and was surprised by what many Christians believed. It was shocking to see how far the church had strayed from the simplicity of Christ.

There is so much confusion in the body of Christ today, with ministers preaching doctrines that are completely contrary to what I discovered in Jesus. To truly understand God, all you need to do is look at Jesus—His words, deeds, actions, reactions, lifestyle, and character. Since I've been born again, there has been only one person I've truly wanted to emulate: Jesus Christ.

If more believers would return to the four Gospels and walk with Jesus from His birth to His resurrection and ascension, much of the confusion in today's church would be dispelled. The reason so many are deceived by false doctrines is that they do not truly know or understand Jesus. As **Hebrews 13:8** reminds us, *"**Jesus Christ the same yesterday, and today, and forever."*** His truth never changes, and it is in Him that we find our foundation.

If we fix our eyes on Christ and His words, much of the noise that surrounds us will fade, leaving only the clarity of His voice guiding us.

# CHAPTER FIVE
## **"Walking with God: Embracing the Abundant Life in Perilous Times"**

Let's look in our Bibles to 2 Timothy chapter 3. We will start there before moving back to the book of Genesis. I want to continue to speak on the simple yet profound subject: **walking with God**. You may not realize it, but this is the very reason we were created. God desires companionship with us, to walk hand in hand with Him, and that's what it means to walk with God. As **John 10:10 (KJV)** says, *"The thief cometh not, but for to steal, and to kill, and to destroy: I am come that they might have life, and that they might have it more abundantly."* This abundant life is found in walking with God.

From the beginning, God intended for us to walk with Him. **Genesis 3:8** tells us, *"And they heard the voice of the LORD God walking in the garden in the cool of the day."* Even after humanity sinned, God sought to walk with us. But the enemy, Satan, does everything in his power to separate us from this divine fellowship. The times we are living in now, as Paul prophesied in **2**

**Timothy 3:1**, are dangerous and perilous for Christians. Yet, these dangers are not just physical disasters like earthquakes or political upheavals. The real danger lies in the moral decay of the human heart.

I am 68 years old, and in my lifetime, I have witnessed the fulfillment of these prophecies. There was a time when it was rare for children to disobey their parents. Divorce was uncommon in my community, and families stayed together. I grew up outside of Chicago in a small town called Mukwonago, near the Wisconsin border. Back then, I didn't know anyone personally who had been through a divorce. But now, In the United States, about 40% to 50% of marriages end in divorce. This rate varies depending on factors such as age, education, and socioeconomic status. Divorce rates for subsequent marriages are higher, with around 60% of second marriages and 73% of third marriages ending in divorce. Many children are being raised in single-parent homes.

This is not a condemnation of anyone's situation, but it is evidence that we are living in the last days, as Jesus warned in **Matthew 24. 2 Timothy 3:2-3** describes people becoming *"**lovers of their own selves, covetous, boasters, proud, blasphemers, disobedient to parents, unthankful, unholy.**"* This self-love is the foundation of much of the chaos we see in our world today. People love themselves more than they love their families, neighbors, or even God.

Materialism is rampant, and covetousness has gripped many hearts. It's not about having things; it's about never being satisfied. As the Bible reminds us in **1 Timothy**

**6:8, *"And having food and raiment let us be therewith content."*** We brought nothing into this world, and we can take nothing out. When we stand before God, we won't carry any of our earthly possessions with us.

In these perilous times, it's crucial that we return to the heart of what it means to walk with God. It means setting aside our desires for worldly things and seeking first the kingdom of God and His righteousness **(Matthew 6:33).** Just as Enoch walked with God and was taken before the judgment, we too are called to walk in close fellowship with Him, trusting in His promise of eternal life. Let us not be distracted by the materialism or selfishness of this world, but instead, let us focus on walking with our Lord, hand in hand, day by day.

## **"Living in the Last Days: Walking with God in Perilous Times"**

We live in times where the warnings given in scripture about the last days are becoming increasingly evident. Let's turn our focus to **2 Timothy 3:2-4 (KJV),** which describes the moral decay we are witnessing: *"For men shall be lovers of their own selves, covetous, boasters, proud, blasphemers, disobedient to parents, unthankful, unholy, without natural affection..."* These words ring true today as we observe the increasing pride and selfishness in society.

A clear example of this pride is the increase in disrespect, both in families and institutions. I can honestly say that, even when I was a sinner, I never spoke disrespectfully to my father. The reverence I held for him remained until the day he passed. However, in many so-called Christian homes today, children speak disrespectfully to their parents without hesitation. This growing disrespect is also seen in the military, where, in the past, disrespect towards commanding officers was unheard of. In my time serving in 1973, such behavior would have landed someone in serious trouble. Now, it's become common, reflecting a broader shift in attitudes.

This decline in respect and the rise of unthankfulness and unholiness extends even to the way life itself is viewed. Abortion is one such sign of this lack of natural affection, where even the unborn are treated without love or care. **2 Timothy 3:3** speaks of being *"**without natural affection, trucebreakers, false accusers, incontinent, fierce, despisers of those that are good.**"* Trust is broken easily, and people are consumed with their own desires for pleasure, spending more on entertainment than they invest in their walk with God.

The shocking part of this prophecy is that it applies not just to the world but to the church. Many who claim to be walking with God are distracted by materialism and entertainment, loving the pleasures of this world more than they love God. **Revelations 3:17 (KJV)** echoes this sentiment: *"**Because thou sayest, I am rich, and increased with goods, and have need of nothing; and knowest not that thou art wretched, and miserable, and poor, and blind, and naked.**"*

In my early years as a believer, back in 1975, I remember how real the return of Christ felt to us. One morning, as a young pastor, I woke up and couldn't find my wife. Fear filled my heart, and I thought, "Has the rapture happened?" That urgency, that deep expectation of Christ's return, shaped our lives. We knew that walking with God meant not just hearing His Word, but doing it. **James 1:22 (KJV)** warns us, *"**But be ye doers of the word, and not hearers only, deceiving your own selves.**"* The danger of self-deception is real, especially in these perilous times.

We must ask ourselves: Are we truly walking with God, or have we become distracted by the pleasures and comforts of this world? The return of Christ is closer now than ever, and we must be vigilant. Walking with God requires more than a profession of faith—it requires daily action, living in obedience to His Word.

## ** "Walking with God: Rediscovering Our Divine Purpose in a Distracted World"**

In these times, there seems to be little concern for Christ's return, just as it was prophesied. **2 Timothy 3:4 (KJV)** tells us that people would become *"**lovers of pleasures more than lovers of God.**"* This prophecy is unfolding before our eyes. Many claim to have faith, but they deny the power of God to overcome sin in their lives. It's not uncommon to hear the message that sin doesn't matter because *"the blood of Jesus covered it all—past, present, and future."* Yet the Bible clearly teaches that we have the power to overcome sin. As it says in **Romans 6:14 (KJV), *"For sin shall not have dominion over you: for ye are not under the law, but under grace."*** The grace of God empowers us to walk in obedience, not as an excuse to continue in disobedience.

The warning in **2 Timothy 3:5 (KJV)** is sobering: ***"Having a form of godliness, but denying the power thereof: from such turn away."*** This command is challenging because many around us, even in the church, fit this description. But we are called to walk with God, and walking with God is simpler than we often make it. While our flesh resists, and the enemy seeks to steal, kill, and destroy **(John 10:10 KJV),** God created us for one central purpose: companionship.

From the beginning, God desired to walk with humanity. When Adam and Eve sinned, **Genesis 3:8 (KJV)** tells us, ***"And they heard the voice of the LORD God walking in the garden in the cool of the day."*** God Himself was walking in the garden, seeking fellowship with His creation. Even after their disobedience, God's desire for companionship had not changed. This is an essential truth—God created us not because He needs us, but because He desires to have fellowship with us.

You see, we weren't made for our intelligence, our looks, or our personalities. We were made to be companions for God, to share an intimate relationship with Him. While God is completely sufficient in Himself—He has existed eternally without any need—He chose to create us for this divine companionship. We were made to walk with God.

Marriage, in a way, reflects this same kind of intimacy. Sadly, the concept of marriage has shifted and become distorted over time, just as our understanding of walking with God has. The essence of both is companionship, a close, enduring relationship built on love, trust, and shared purpose.

God's actions in Genesis show us something profound about His character. Even though He is omnipresent, capable of being anywhere at any moment, He chooses to walk. It is symbolic of His desire to move with us, to walk alongside us in every moment of life. God's practicality and personal approach to humanity amaze me. He doesn't need to "beam" Himself anywhere, yet He chooses to walk with us in a relatable and meaningful way.

In conclusion, walking with God is our ultimate purpose. It's not complicated, but it does require surrendering the distractions and desires of the world. Let us remember that we were made for intimacy with God, and in every step, He is walking with us, guiding us back to His heart.

## **"The Walk of Faith: Embracing Intimacy with God"**

In many ways, walking holds deep symbolic meaning in our lives, especially when it comes to our relationship with God. As we read in **Genesis 3:8 (KJV), *"And they heard the voice of the LORD God walking in the**

**garden in the cool of the day."*** From the beginning, God has desired to walk with His creation. Even Jesus walked on water, as described in **Matthew 14:25 (KJV),** demonstrating not only His divine authority but also His personal desire for connection. God enjoys walking, and this act represents a profound time of intimacy and closeness.

Think about how meaningful it is to take a walk with family members. When you're walking hand in hand with someone—especially with a spouse or your children—it's a time of shared experiences, conversation, and growing together. My wife and I had often walked through the mall on snowy or rainy days, holding hands as we strolled along. This simple act strengthened our bond, reminding us of our connection. Walking symbolizes closeness, just as holding hands does with your child, signifying that deep, loving relationship.

For me, walking with God is much like those walks with my family—it's intimate and personal. Growing up, we didn't know Christ, but even without understanding the spiritual significance, my family still spent time walking together. We would take long walks down dirt roads, picking asparagus and enjoying each other's company. Those walks brought us closer, just as walking with God brings us closer to Him. Walking is more than just movement—it represents relationship, growth, and learning together.

When we study the Bible, we see how often walking is mentioned. There are nearly 400 scriptures dealing with walking, many of which reference walking with God.

One key scripture is **Deuteronomy 10:12 (KJV)**, *"**And now, Israel, what doth the LORD thy God require of thee, but to fear the LORD thy God, to walk in all his ways, and to love him, and to serve the LORD thy God with all thy heart and with all thy soul."*** Walking with God is central to our purpose—He created us for companionship with Him.

Our two legs and feet were given to us for more than just physical movement—they were given to us to walk with the Lord. Walking with God is about learning, growing, and spending time in His presence. Sometimes, during these spiritual walks, we pause, we sit, and we listen. My father, though he didn't know the Lord, used to take us on those long walks and speak to us children. It was in those moments that we grew as a family, and I now see that walking with God has the same effect in my spiritual life.

Prayer, I believe, is much like this walk. It's an intimate time spent in conversation with God. We were created for this very purpose—to walk with the Lord, hand in hand, through the journey of life. The same way I hold my wife's hand as we walk is how I hold onto God through prayer and trust. **Psalm 23:4 (KJV)** beautifully reminds us, *"**Yea, though I walk through the valley of the shadow of death, I will fear no evil: for thou art with me; thy rod and thy staff they comfort me."*** Walking with God means He is with us through every season of life.

In conclusion, walking with God is not only our purpose but also our privilege. Whether through prayer, meditation, or simply reflecting on His Word, we are invited to walk hand in hand with our Creator, experiencing the fullness of His presence in our lives. Let us cherish every step, knowing we are never walking alone.

## **\*"Walking with God: A Journey of Intimacy, Learning, and Agreement"\*\***

Walking with God is not just a concept; it's a daily journey, a profound act of connection. It's something we are meant to experience throughout our lives. In **Genesis 3:8 (KJV)**, we read, *"**And they heard the voice of the LORD God walking in the garden in the cool of the day."*** God desires that same closeness with us, a walk of intimacy where we learn and grow together.

When I was a child, there was a saying: *"Children should be seen and not heard."* While I don't fully agree with that, I do believe that sometimes there's too much noise, especially from children. They can miss out on learning from those who've walked much farther along in life. Life is a journey, and walking through it is the only way to gain experience. As the Bible teaches in **James 1:22 (KJV), *"But be ye doers of the word, and not hearers only, deceiving your own selves."*** Walking with God means putting His word into action, not just talking about it.

For me, prayer is one of the most meaningful ways to walk with God. I've found that when I walk and pray,

God speaks to me the most. It's not just about me talking to God, it's about listening to Him. It's in those quiet moments, walking with the Lord, that He reveals His wisdom to me. As it says in **Amos 3:3 (KJV), *"Can two walk together, except they be agreed?"*** Walking with God requires agreement with His ways, His word, and His will.

Walking is also a physical activity that involves every part of us—our muscles, our energy, our attention. The average person walks about 115,000 miles in their lifetime. Imagine if every step we took was in step with God, fully engaged in His presence. Jesus, when He called His disciples, simply said, ***"Follow me."*** What He was really saying was, ***"Walk with me."*** Walking with God is the same call today. It's not about multitasking; it's about focusing on the One who walks beside us, just as a loved one walks hand in hand with you.

I remember hearing a beautiful Christian song some years ago about a man who walked his wife home, both literally and figuratively. The song tells the story of a young man who walked his wife home after dates, then walked with her through life—raising children, becoming grandparents—and eventually, as she lay on her deathbed, he was there walking her to her final home in heaven passing away with her at her side in the hospital. That song always brings me to tears because it's such a touching reminder of the closeness of walking through life together, and it mirrors how we should walk with God every day. Just as that man walked with his wife until the very end, God desires to walk with us all the way home, to eternity.

However, walking together is only possible when there's agreement. As **Amos 3:3** says, two cannot walk together unless they are in harmony. This truth reflects in relationships, too. Divorce, for example, is often the result of two people no longer walking in agreement. Disagreements, arguments, and conflicts make it difficult to walk side by side. But when there's unity, walking together becomes effortless and fulfilling. It's the same with God—if we're constantly at odds with His will or His word, we can't walk with Him.

Just as Adam and Eve *"**heard the voice of the LORD God walking in the garden**"*, we are called to hear His voice and walk with Him today. It's in these quiet walks with God that we find peace, direction, and the strength to carry on. Walking with God isn't just about where we are going, it's about who we are walking with, and the intimacy and love shared along the way.

In conclusion, walking with God is an invitation to intimacy, learning, and agreement. As we walk through life, may we remember that every step is an opportunity to grow closer to our Creator, who desires to walk with us through every moment and every season. Let us walk in unity with Him, knowing that He will walk us all the way home

# God's presence disappears. God where are you?

In our walk with God, there are many things that we absolutely must learn. I wish that we could instantly learn them just from reading the Bible, but this is not the case. I had to learn a very hard lesson early in my Christian walk that many who have walked with God for years still have not learned. I believe the reason I had to learn this lesson was because of the number of trials, tests and hardships that I was about to experience throughout my lifetime. I had to learn how to not live by feelings or by the circumstances that surrounded me.

I gave my heart to Christ on February 18th, 1975. The reality of Christ came rushing inside of me like a mighty ocean of life. My whole life before had been filled with pain, sorrow, depression, low self-esteem, physical disabilities, etc. You name it, I had it. But when I gave my heart to Christ, the presence of God instantly overwhelmed me. It was like electricity going through my body 24 hours a day, seven days a week. This did not go away but continued upon me.

I instantly was set free from all addictions as well as my emotional and mental problems. I was a brand-new creation in Christ Jesus. I fell in love with my Lord Head over heels. I immediately began devouring the Word of the Living God, specifically the four Gospels. I got filled with the Holy Ghost, healed and preached my first sermon very shortly after I was saved. I think that I took the presence and the touch of God upon my life for granted at that time, as if that was the normal everyday experience for every believer. I was soon to discover this was not true.

One morning I got up early to pray and to read my Bible as normal, but something was wrong. I had grown used to the very tangible presence and manifestation of God but, to my shock and horror, it was gone. I mean to me personally; the presence of God was gone. Confusion suddenly clouded my heart and my mind. I cried out to God, "Lord, what's wrong. How have I offended you?" I did not hear any answer which was, to me, also very strange. The Lord was constantly speaking to my heart. I examined myself to see if there was something I was doing that was against the will of God. I could not find anything wrong.

I didn't know what else to do and I didn't really have anyone that I could go to at that time who was mature enough to help me. So, I kept reading my bible, kept on praying, worshipping, praising, and sharing Christ as I went along. I went to bed that night with no sense of God's presence.

The next morning, I got up early hoping that His presence had come back, but to my shock and sadness, God was not there. Once again, I went through the torment of examining my heart, crying out to Jesus and following my regular routine throughout the day. I went to bed that night in the same condition. Now, during this whole experience, I did not back off or give up but just kept pressing on.

This went on day after day after day. God just was not there in His tangible presence. Yes, I did get depressed, but I did not give up. I did not stop praying or reading my bible. I never ceased worshiping and praising God. I did not stop sharing my faith with others and telling them the wonderful things Jesus had done for me. I think approximately two weeks went by with me in this spiritual desert —a no man's land— a dark and dry place in my daily walk.

I did not know what was wrong but there was nothing else I could do but to keep pressing closer. After about two weeks, I went to bed one night praying and talking to God even though he was not answering me in the same way as He did before.

The next morning, I got up early once again and began to pray when, out of the blue, God's presence came rushing in stronger than ever like a mighty wind. It was like a powerful tsunami, a forceful flood of His presence and His Spirit. God's touch was upon me greatly. I began to laugh, to cry and to shout. Oh, it was so good to have God with me again. I said to the Lord when I was finally able to talk, "Lord, where were you?"

There seemed to be a long pause, then He said to me with what seemed to be a bit of amusement in His voice, "I Was Here All along." You were, Lord? Yes, He replied. And then he said something that was to forever change my life. "I was teaching you how to live by faith." He then began to very specifically teach me out of the scriptures that man does not live by bread alone but by every word that comes out of the mouth of God.

I learned that our walk with Him does not depend upon our feelings, emotions, location or circumstance and that many of those who are believers are destroyed by the enemy because they do not understand nor believe this. Even the apostle Paul had to learn how to be content in Christ in whatever condition, trusting God, knowing that He is not a man that He should lie. Christ has said that he would never leave us nor forsake us. We may call upon Christ with a sincere heart knowing that He will be there for us to answer us and to show us great and mighty things which we know not!

Over 49 years have come and gone since I learned this lesson. I now no longer allow the feelings of either His absence or His presence to affect me. Of course, I constantly examine my heart but if I can find nothing wrong, I simply realize that I am flying by instruments, no longer operating by visual flight rules (VFR).

Thank God, as the aviation industry would say, I am SFR rated! There are two sets of regulations governing all aspects of civilian aircraft operations: the first is Instrument flight rules (IFR) and the second is visual flight rules (VFR) defined as flying by sight and sensory input. All Christians are to be rated as (SFR) which would equate to Spiritual Flight Rules!

**Romans 4:18 Who against hope believed in hope, that he might become the father of many nations; according to that which was spoken, So shall thy seed be.**

# CHAPTER SIX
## **"Walking with God: A Life of Faith and Divine Companionship"**

As we delve into the profound act of walking with God, it is essential to recognize that this concept goes beyond physical movement—it's about a spiritual journey. In **Genesis 3:8 (KJV),** we read, *"And they heard the voice of the LORD God walking in the garden in the cool of the day."* God wasn't just strolling; He was speaking, communicating His heart to Adam and Eve. In the same way, Jesus invited His apostles to *"follow me,"* which was an invitation to walk with Him both physically and spiritually.

Jesus could have chosen horses or chariots for His journey, but instead, He walked. He did this because walking together symbolizes closeness and intimacy. For three and a half years, the disciples walked alongside Jesus, learning to walk not just in the flesh but in the spirit. As **Galatians 5:16 (KJV)** tells us, *"Walk in the Spirit, and ye shall not fulfill the lust of the flesh."* Walking in the Spirit means aligning ourselves with God's will, staying in agreement with His Word, and refusing to follow the distractions of the world.

This world offers countless paths: Hollywood, sports, materialism, and even foolishness. If we love these things, we will find ourselves walking hand in hand with them. However, if we love Jesus and spiritual truths, we will walk with Him and those who share the same love. **Amos 3:3 (KJV)** asks, *"Can two walk together, except they be agreed?"* To walk with God means to walk in agreement with His ways, to be a doer of His Word **(James 1:22 KJV),** and to forsake the ways of the world.

In the days of Noah, only a few walked with God. Among them was Enoch, who did not start his walk with the Lord until he was over 60 years old. Before then, Enoch lived like many others—surviving, getting by, but not truly walking with God. Something stirred within him, and he realized that walking with the world, the flesh, and society had left him empty. He longed for something more. **Hebrews 11:5 (KJV)** tells us, *"By faith Enoch was translated that he should not see death; and was not found, because God had translated him: for before his translation he had this testimony, that he pleased God."* Enoch chose to walk with God, and it was by faith that he pleased Him.

The Bible only mentions twelve men who pleased God—Enoch and Jesus. While many others certainly walked by faith and lived righteous lives, as detailed in Hebrews 11, the specific testimony of pleasing God was reserved for few men. Walking with God requires faith, as **Hebrews 11:6 (KJV)** reminds us, *"But without faith it is

**impossible to please him."*** Faith is the foundation of our walk, and it is through faith that we grow closer to God.

In conclusion, walking with God is a journey that requires faith, obedience, and a willingness to forsake worldly distractions. Just as Enoch chose to turn from the ways of the world and walk with God, we too can make that choice today. As we walk in faith, we will find the fulfillment, peace, and intimacy with God that we were created for.

Several men in the Bible are mentioned as having pleased God. Below is a list of individuals along with corresponding KJV scriptures that describe their actions, faith, and relationship with God, which led to them being seen as pleasing to Him.

1. **Enoch**
   - **Scripture**: *"**By faith Enoch was translated that he should not see death; and was not found, because God had translated him: for before his translation he had this testimony, that he pleased God."*** (Hebrews 11:5, KJV)

Enoch is explicitly mentioned as having pleased God, and as a result, he was taken up to heaven without experiencing death.

2. **Jesus Christ**
   - **Scripture**: *"**And lo a voice from heaven, saying, This is my beloved Son, in whom I am well pleased."*** (Matthew 3:17, KJV)

God declares His pleasure in His Son, Jesus Christ, multiple times during His ministry, affirming that Jesus lived a life fully pleasing to God.

3. **Abraham**
- **Scripture**: *"And the scripture was fulfilled which saith, Abraham believed God, and it was imputed unto him for righteousness: and he was called the Friend of God."* (James 2:23, KJV)

Abraham's faith pleased God, and his trust in God's promises was counted as righteousness.

4. **Noah**
- **Scripture**: *"But Noah found grace in the eyes of the LORD."* (Genesis 6:8, KJV)
- **Scripture**: *"By faith Noah, being warned of God of things not seen as yet, moved with fear, prepared an ark to the saving of his house; by the which he condemned the world, and became heir of the righteousness which is by faith."* (Hebrews 11:7, KJV)

Noah's faith and obedience to God's command to build the ark saved him and his family, and this pleased God.

5. **David**
- **Scripture**: *"And when he had removed him, he raised up unto them David to be their king; to whom also he gave testimony, and said, I have found David the son of Jesse, a man after mine own heart, which shall fulfil all my will."* (Acts 13:22, KJV)

David is described as a man after God's own heart, which implies that his life and leadership were pleasing to God, even though he had moments of failure.

6. **Solomon (early life)**
   - **Scripture**: *"And the speech pleased the Lord, that Solomon had asked this thing."* (1 Kings 3:10, KJV)

Early in his reign, Solomon's request for wisdom to lead God's people pleased the Lord.

7. **Samuel**
   - **Scripture**: *"And Samuel grew, and the LORD was with him, and did let none of his words fall to the ground."* (1 Samuel 3:19, KJV)

Samuel's faithfulness and dedication to God's work from his youth pleased the Lord.

8. **Hezekiah**
   - **Scripture**: *"And he did that which was right in the sight of the LORD, according to all that David his father did."* (2 Kings 18:3, KJV)

King Hezekiah's faithfulness and reforms during his reign pleased God as he turned the people back to worshiping the Lord.

9. **Elijah**
   - **Scripture**: *"And Elijah the Tishbite, who was of the inhabitants of Gilead, said unto Ahab, As the

**LORD God of Israel liveth, before whom I stand, there shall not be dew nor rain these years, but according to my word."\*** (1 Kings 17:1, KJV)

Elijah's unwavering faith and boldness in speaking the word of God before kings and leading Israel away from idolatry were acts that pleased God.

10. **Job**
- **Scripture**: *"**And the LORD said unto Satan, Hast thou considered my servant Job, that there is none like him in the earth, a perfect and an upright man, one that feareth God, and escheweth evil?"\*** (Job 1:8, KJV)

Job's faithfulness, even under extreme suffering, was acknowledged and praised by God.

11. **Daniel**
- **Scripture**: *"**Then said Daniel unto the king, O king, live for ever. My God hath sent his angel, and hath shut the lions' mouths, that they have not hurt me: forasmuch as before him innocency was found in me; and also before thee, O king, have I done no hurt."\*** (Daniel 6:21-22, KJV)

Daniel's unwavering faith and trust in God, even in the face of death, pleased God, and he was spared in the lion's den.

12. **Caleb and Joshua**
- **Scripture**: *"**But my servant Caleb, because he had another spirit with him, and hath followed me

fully, him will I bring into the land whereinto he went; and his seed shall possess it."* (Numbers 14:24, KJV)

- **Scripture**: *"Only rebel not ye against the LORD, neither fear ye the people of the land; for they are bread for us: their defence is departed from them, and the LORD is with us: fear them not."* (Numbers 14:9, KJV)

Caleb and Joshua pleased God by their faith and courage when they stood against the other spies and encouraged Israel to trust in God's promise.

---

These men pleased God through faith, obedience, and righteousness. They serve as examples for believers today, reminding us that *"without faith it is impossible to please him"* (Hebrews 11:6, KJV).

## **"Learning to Walk: A Spiritual Journey from Crawling to Running with God"**

Humans, unlike many animals, experience a slower process of learning to walk. While animals like horses are able to stand and move almost immediately after birth, humans begin by crawling before they can eventually stand and walk on two feet. This natural progression reflects a deeper spiritual journey that every believer must undergo as they grow in their walk with God.

Consider the fascinating behavior of horse foals. Within an hour or two of being born, they are already on their feet, walking, and learning to run. This immediate mobility is crucial for their survival in the wild, where predators are a constant threat. Their strong instinct to stand, follow their mothers, and navigate their surroundings showcases the importance of early development.

Foals have to learn how to use their muscles and legs rapidly, but their coordination improves over time. While they can run almost immediately, it takes a few days for them to master control and gain confidence. The early stages of this growth are key, and it's a powerful metaphor for how we, as believers, begin our spiritual walk.

In the same way, children learn to walk by watching their parents. If the parents don't know how to walk, or if there's no one around to guide them, it would take much longer for a child to learn. Parents, especially with their first child, are eager to see them walk as early as possible. Some even feel anxious if their child isn't walking by nine months. However, by the time parents have multiple children, they become more patient and allow the process to unfold naturally. There's no need to rush, as each child will walk in their own time.

In the spiritual realm, the same principle applies. We often feel the need to rush our growth in faith. We want to mature quickly, learn everything, and achieve all of our spiritual goals right away. But God is never in a hurry. **Isaiah 40:31 (KJV)** reminds us, ***"But they that wait upon the LORD shall renew their strength; they shall mount up with wings as eagles; they shall run, and not be weary; and they shall walk, and not faint."*** Growth in the Lord takes time and patience.

I remember watching my son, Michael, as a child. He fell so often that I almost wanted to tell him to stay on the floor for a while and give his head a rest! But those falls were a part of his learning process. Just like in our spiritual journey, we start by crawling. At first, we may drag ourselves along, just learning to move forward in small ways. As we grow, we start to stand, but we fall—often. Yet, those falls are not failures. They are lessons that help us to become stronger in our faith.

I see this in little boy, who loves to jump. He jumps a few times and then falls, landing on his bottom, but he keeps getting up. His persistence mirrors our desire to grow in our walk with God. We want to run, jump, and soar in our spiritual lives, but we must first learn the basics—how to walk steadily with the Lord. **Galatians 5:25 (KJV) reminds us, *"If we live in the Spirit, let us also walk in the Spirit."*** Walking in the Spirit takes time and practice, just like learning to walk as a child.

Parents who know how to walk in the Spirit can guide their children on the same path. However, if a parent doesn't know how to walk in faith, it becomes difficult for their children to learn. That's why it's so crucial for families to grow together in their faith journey. **Proverbs 22:6 (KJV) instructs, *"Train up a child in the way he should go: and when he is old, he will not depart from**

**it."*** Our spiritual walk doesn't happen overnight, and it requires guidance, patience, and a steady commitment to learning and growing in the Lord.

In conclusion, just as children learn to walk by watching their parents, we too must learn to walk with God by following His example and trusting in His guidance. Spiritual growth takes time, and there's no need to rush the process. Whether we are crawling, standing, or running, we are on a journey of faith, learning to walk hand in hand with the Lord every step of the way.

# **"Walking in the Spirit: A Journey at God's Pace"**

Walking in the Spirit is a step-by-step journey with God, where we grow in faith and avoid fulfilling the desires of the flesh. **Galatians 5:16 (KJV) says, *"This I say then, Walk in the Spirit, and ye shall not fulfil the lust of the flesh."*** But how can we expect our children to walk in the Spirit if we, as parents, aren't walking in the Spirit ourselves?

As I reflect on how we interact with the animals in our lives, I can't help but notice the similarity between how we talk to them and how God communicates with us. For example, many of us have pets, like dogs or horses, and we often speak to them as if they understand every word. A sister in Christ I know talks to her horses, gently patting them and saying, *"Hey, Sassy, how you doing?"* It's a tender interaction, and just like that, I believe God speaks to all of creation. In fact, **Zephaniah 3:17 (KJV) says, *"The LORD thy God in the midst of thee is mighty; he will save, he will rejoice over thee with joy; he will rest in his love, he will joy over thee with singing."*** God not only speaks but sings over His creation, including us.

For three and a half years, Jesus' disciples walked with Him, listening to His teachings and learning from His every word. That's the essence of Christianity—walking with God, not rushing to get somewhere or accomplish something. God isn't in a hurry; He desires to walk with us, to spend time with us. When we are in tune with His pace, spiritual growth becomes a natural part of our daily walk. Enoch, for example, walked with God for 300 years, and **Genesis 5:24 (KJV) tells us, *"And Enoch walked with God: and he was not; for God took him."*** This walk is a long-term, one-step-at-a-time journey.

I'll admit, I've always been in a hurry, especially when walking with my family. My children will tell you that I walk too fast, always eager to get in and out of stores or to move on to the next task. My wife, on the other hand, enjoys the experience of walking. She likes to take her time, looking at everything, touching things as she goes along—she's in no rush. It's easy to see how frustrating it can be when one person is moving fast and the other is slow. Yet, this is how we often are with God. We either try to rush ahead of Him, or we lag behind.

When we walk as a family, I like us all to stay together.

But there's always one who gets ahead—Steven. He'll race ahead a mile, and I find myself calling out, *"Steven, come back here! We're losing the whole point of walking together!"* Then there's Danny, who drags his feet, and I have to nudge him along, saying, *"Move it, boy, move it!"* Walking together requires finding a common pace, just like enjoying a cup of coffee. You don't want to drink it too fast and burn yourself, but you also don't want to let it get cold. You've got to savor the experience.

Spiritually, walking with God is the same. We need to find His pace and stay in step with Him. Sometimes we get ahead of God, thinking we know the way, but when we rush, we miss the beauty of the journey. Other times, we drag behind, reluctant to move forward, and we need God's gentle nudge to keep us going. The key is to stay in sync with His timing, knowing that He's not in a rush, but He's also not idle.

In conclusion, walking with God is not about speed but about staying in step with Him. Just like walking as a family, we need to find the rhythm that allows us to enjoy the journey together. Whether we're tempted to rush ahead or drag our feet, the important thing is to keep walking with the Lord, trusting His pace and savoring the moments we share with Him.

## **"Walking with God: Embracing the Journey Together"**

God desires for us to walk with Him, not just in this life but throughout eternity. If you don't enjoy walking with God now, how will you embrace the endless journey in heaven? Walking with God isn't about rushing from place to place but about absorbing all He has to offer and growing in fellowship with Him. Before sin entered the world, walking with God was a part of life, and it will be again in the perfect world to come. **Genesis 3:8 (KJV)** reminds us, *"**And they heard the voice of the LORD God walking in the garden in the cool of the day."*** This is what we were created for—communion with our Creator.

Marriage is a beautiful reflection of this divine walk. God designed marriage for companionship, not merely for practical arrangements like having children or sharing finances. The true purpose of marriage is to enjoy one another's company, just as we were made to enjoy God's presence. **Ephesians 5:31-32 (KJV)** tells us, *"**For this cause shall a man leave his father and mother, and shall be joined unto his wife, and they two shall be one flesh. This is a great mystery: but I speak concerning Christ and the church."*** Marriage, like our relationship with God, is about walking together, growing closer with each step.

I've often asked couples, *"Why did you marry?"* and sometimes the answers surprise me. Some married for practical reasons, while others felt pressured or desperate. But marriage, at its heart, is about enjoying each other, just as God enjoys walking with us. Personally, after over 45 years of marriage, I still love spending time with my wife, though I sometimes have to persuade her to slow down and walk with me. This is the same relationship God seeks with us—He wants us to slow down and walk with Him.

God speaks to us in ways we can understand, coming down to our level just as we speak gently to children. How often do we, as parents, ask our children questions we already know the answers to? We do it not because we need their answers, but because we want to interact with them. In the same way, God engages with us, asking questions and drawing us into relationship. In **Job 38:4 (KJV)**, God asked, *"**Where wast thou when I laid the foundations of the earth?"*** Of course, God knew the answer, but He invites us to engage with Him, to think, to converse, and to grow.

Jesus did the same when He became a man. He came down to our level, experiencing our struggles and weaknesses. **Hebrews 4:15 (KJV) tells us,** *"**For we have not an high priest which cannot be touched with the feeling of our infirmities; but was in all points tempted like as we are, yet without sin."*** Jesus walked among us, teaching us how to walk with God. His life shows that God meets us where we are, gently leading us into deeper fellowship.

When we look at the story of Martha and Mary in **Luke 10:38-42,** we see two different approaches to walking with God. Martha was busy, consumed with tasks, while Mary chose to sit at Jesus' feet, listening and learning. Jesus said of Mary, *"**But one thing is needful: and Mary hath chosen that good part, which shall not be taken away from her."*** **(Luke 10:42, KJV).** Walking with God doesn't mean you have to be physically moving—it's about being in His presence, just like Mary did. And no one can take that relationship away from you.

Those who don't walk with God may try to discourage you, but your journey with Him is yours alone. **Psalm 91:1 (KJV)** tells us, *"**He that dwelleth in the secret place of the most High shall abide under the shadow of the Almighty."*** Walking with God is the safest, most fulfilling place to be. It's under His shadow, where we find peace, guidance, and protection.

In conclusion, walking with God is about companionship, just as marriage reflects our walk with Him. It's not about rushing but about taking the time to enjoy His presence, learning from Him, and allowing Him to guide our steps. Whether in marriage or our spiritual journey, we are made to walk together in love and unity. So, start your walk with God today and let it continue throughout eternity

# Truskowski Tries to Stab Me to Death

Not long after being born again, I felt a strong urge in my heart to reach out to the group of young men I used to run with just outside of Chicago. We weren't a formal gang with a name or initiation rituals, but we were constantly involved in corrupt activities—drinking, fighting, using drugs, stripping cars, and worse. One day, I found myself sitting in a car between two of the main instigators of our trouble: Gary and Claire. Both of these men were large and muscular, intimidating figures.

I passionately shared Christ with them and the others, testifying to how much God had transformed my life. While they sat around drinking, using dope, and cussing, I explained that I was on a heavenly high that no drug or worldly experience could match. Most of them just stared at me, unsure of how to react. They knew the old Mike Yeager, the one who had been deep in sin, addicted to drugs and alcohol. They had seen me at my worst. But now, I was a new creation in Christ, filled with an overwhelming zeal to preach the good news.

Gary, however, was different from the others in a much darker way. He had always been volatile, like a stick of dynamite ready to explode. Having already spent time behind bars, he harbored a deep, seething hatred toward me—one that I didn't fully understand until it surfaced in a moment of terrifying violence.

We were driving out of Racine, Illinois, with Gary behind the wheel and Claire sitting against the passenger door. I was in the middle. Without warning, Gary reached for a large knife lodged in the old steel dashboard of the car. With his right hand, he pulled the knife free, raised it high in the air, and brought it down toward my stomach with incredible force.

At that moment, I entered into what I can only describe as the realm of the Spirit, where time seems to slow down. The knife came down in slow motion, and I saw my hands reaching up to grab Gary's wrist, diverting the blade away from my gut and into the seat. His thrust was so powerful that the knife pierced right through the car seat. But he wasn't done. Gary pulled the knife out of the seat and tried to stab me again, all while driving down the road.

Each time he drove the knife toward me, I managed to divert the blade, narrowly avoiding injury to my legs and private areas. During the entire ordeal, the peace of God overwhelmed me. My heart wasn't racing, nor was I shaking with fear. Instead, I felt as though I were in heaven. The presence of God was so powerful and supernatural that I couldn't help but marvel at how He was delivering me from this madman.

As Gary continued his attack, a police car suddenly appeared ahead of us. When Gary saw the officer, he threw the knife out of the car window. Without a word, he kept driving, and Claire, who I once thought was a friend, did nothing to help me. Yet, throughout the entire situation, God's peace remained upon me like an invisible blanket.

*"**Thou wilt keep him in perfect peace, whose mind is stayed on thee: because he trusteth in thee**"* (**Isaiah 26:3, KJV**). That day, God's perfect peace carried me through a situation where death seemed imminent.

# Truskowski Shoots Me with a Shotgun

Just two days after Gary tried to stab me, I found myself at his house once again. I knew I shouldn't have gone there, especially after what had just happened, but something drew me back. As I pulled up in my sister's red Maverick, Gary was sitting on his porch. When he saw me, he grabbed a shotgun that had been leaning against the house.

As I walked toward him, he aimed the shotgun right at my stomach. There was no fear in my heart, not even a flicker. I just kept walking toward him. When I was about twenty feet away, the barrel of the gun jerked slightly to the right as he pulled the trigger. The sound of the shot echoed through the valley.

Miraculously, nothing happened to me. As I think back on that day, I firmly believe an angel nudged the gun just enough to save my life. Whether the gun was loaded with birdshot or a deer slug, I felt nothing. The shot must have missed me by mere inches. Once again, I wasn't shaken, my heart wasn't racing, and it felt as though I were walking in heaven.

I calmly walked up the steps of the porch, took the gun out of Gary's hands, and leaned it back against the house. He just stared at me, speechless. That was the last time I ever saw Gary, and to this day, I have no idea what became of him.

**\*"No weapon that is formed against thee shall prosper; and every tongue that shall rise against thee in judgment thou shalt condemn. This is the heritage of the servants of the LORD, and their righteousness**

**is of me, saith the LORD"\* (Isaiah 54:17, KJV).**

Through both of these encounters, I witnessed the power of God's protection firsthand. His peace and presence surrounded me in the midst of danger, and no weapon formed against me was able to prosper.

# CHAPTER SEVEN
## **"Walking with God: The Simplicity of Divine Fellowship"**

The beauty of God's creation often mirrors the relationship He desires with us. Just as we see a mother duck leading her ducklings along the pond or puppies following closely behind their mother, we, as God's children, are meant to walk closely with Him. This instinct to follow, to be near, is embedded in creation and serves as a reflection of how we are called to walk with our Creator.

Enoch's story is a powerful example of this closeness. **Genesis 5:24 (KJV)** tells us, ***"And Enoch walked with God: and he was not; for God took him."*** Enoch walked so closely with God that one day, God simply took him home. Every day, Enoch spent time with the Lord, enjoying His presence, walking with Him in the cool of the day, just as Adam once did before sin entered the world. However, when sin came, it separated mankind from God. **Genesis 3:9-10 (KJV)** reveals the moment when God called out to Adam, ***"Adam, where*** art thou?"* Adam responded, *"I heard thy voice in the garden, and I was afraid, because I was naked; and I hid myself."* Sin had broken that intimate walk, leaving man in fear and shame.

But God, in His mercy, made a way to restore that fellowship. He killed a lamb and used its skin to cover Adam's nakedness **(Genesis 3:21, KJV)**, symbolizing the sacrifice that would ultimately come through Jesus Christ. John the Baptist echoed this truth in **John 1:29 (KJV)** when he declared, *"**Behold the Lamb of God, which taketh away the sin of the world.**"* Jesus, the Lamb of God, came to cover our sin and restore us to the walk with God that was lost in the Garden of Eden. God could have created a new race from the rocks, as John the Baptist said **(Matthew 3:9, KJV)**, but His heart was set on us. He wanted to walk with us again, so much so that He was willing to die and rise again to make it possible.

What God desires from us isn't our worldly success or accolades. He isn't impressed by degrees or titles. All He wants is for us to walk with Him. **Micah 6:8 (KJV)** tells us plainly, *"**He hath shewed thee, O man, what is good; and what doth the LORD require of thee, but to do justly, and to love mercy, and to walk humbly with thy God?**"* It's not complicated. God wants a simple, daily walk with us, not hindered by the distractions we often put in the way.

Imagine planning a quiet evening walk with your spouse, but instead of enjoying the moment together, your spouse is preoccupied with getting ready—fixing their hair, adjusting their clothes, worrying about appearances.

Meanwhile, the sun is setting, and the moment is slipping away. You find yourself saying, *"Honey, I don't care about your makeup. I just want to take a walk with you."* This is often how we are with God. We get so caught up in trying to present ourselves perfectly that we forget He just wants to be with us, just as we are.

Walking with God isn't difficult. It's simply a matter of putting one foot in front of the other, taking time to be in His presence, and allowing Him to guide us step by step. It doesn't require perfection or impressive accomplishments—just a heart willing to be near Him.

In conclusion, God's desire is simple—He wants to walk with us. Not in a rushed, hurried way, but in a close, daily relationship where we learn to trust Him with each step. Like a child following their mother or a husband and wife enjoying a peaceful walk together, we are called to walk with God, not weighed down by the world's expectations, but free in His love.

# **"Walking with God: Step by Step in Faith and Love"**

Each moment in our walk with God is like taking a step—whether through scripture, prayer, or worship. Every step draws us closer to Him. **Isaiah 26:3 (KJV) says, *"Thou wilt keep him in perfect peace, whose mind is stayed on thee: because he trusteth in thee."*** When our minds are fixed on God, we are continually walking with Him. However, sin disrupts that walk, as we see in the Garden of Eden when God calls out to Adam, *"**Where art thou?**"* **(Genesis 3:9, KJV)**.

Adam's response is telling. Instead of taking responsibility, he points to Eve, his walking companion, and blames her for his failure. **Genesis 3:12 (KJV)** records his words: *"**The woman whom thou gavest to be with me, she gave me of the tree, and I did eat.**"* This is where division began, fueled by the devil, the accuser of the brethren **(Revelation 12:10, KJV)**. The enemy's goal is to separate us from our companions, just as he separated Adam from Eve in that moment.

When you're in love, the flaws of the other person are often invisible. Love is blind to imperfections. When a couple first falls in love, they hold hands, walk together, and don't focus on each other's shortcomings. But if the enemy can get between you, the first thing he'll try to do is break that bond. If you're married, grab your spouse's hand and hold on tightly. If your spouse isn't walking with God, hold their hand anyway, praying that through your love and godly lifestyle, you might win them to Christ. **1 Peter 3:1 (KJV)** reminds us of this hope: *"**Likewise, ye wives, be in subjection to your own husbands; that, if any obey not the word, they also may without the word be won by the conversation of the wives.**"*

The enemy's work is clear in Genesis 3. He seeks to divide and accuse. But in **Genesis 3:15 (KJV),** God reveals His plan to defeat the devil through the seed of the woman, saying, *"**it shall bruise thy head, and thou shalt bruise his heel.**"* The victory over Satan will come through the foot of man. This imagery is powerful—God's plan for redemption involves us walking in victory over the enemy.

This brings us to the significance of feet in scripture. When Jesus washed His disciples' feet, Peter resisted, saying, *"**Thou shalt never wash my feet."*** But Jesus replied, *"**If I wash thee not, thou hast no part with me."*** **(John 13:8, KJV).** Feet represent the walk of a believer. Once you are born again, walking with God is a moment-by-moment experience. Washing our feet is symbolic of cleansing our daily walk with Him, ensuring that we stay close and connected.

God's desire is for us to walk with Him and with those He has placed in our lives. The enemy will do everything he can to disrupt that walk, whether through division in marriages or distractions that pull us away from God. But the key is to keep walking, step by step, holding on to those we love and staying in fellowship with the Lord.

In conclusion, walking with God is not a one-time event—it's a step-by-step journey. Each prayer, each scripture, each act of love is another step closer to Him. Just as God has planned victory over the enemy through our walk, let us continue walking in faith, love, and unity, both with Him and with those He's placed in our lives.

# **"Walking with God: Savoring Every Step of the Journey"**

Walking with God is much like savoring a meal. Just as I enjoy my steak, rare and full of flavor, cut into small bites to fully appreciate each one, our spiritual journey should be savored slowly, taking in each moment and revelation. We sometimes try to consume too much at once, wanting answers to every question and trying to grasp every concept. But just as you can't rush through a good meal without missing the taste, you can't rush your walk with God without missing His lessons.

When we're born again, we often feel the need to understand everything immediately. We may feel overwhelmed, saying, *"I don't understand this, or that."* But just as children learn one step at a time, asking countless questions along the way, we must also take our time, digesting God's truths bit by bit. **Proverbs 2:6 (KJV) reminds us, *"For the LORD giveth wisdom: out of his mouth cometh knowledge and understanding."*** We don't need to have all the answers right away—God will reveal them in time as we mature in our faith.

Through the years, I've had visions, dreams, and even visitations from God. I've never been confused by them because I trust that, in time, God will reveal their meaning. **Ecclesiastes 3:11 (KJV) tells us, *"He hath made every thing beautiful in his time."*** Sometimes, we get a glimpse of something and want immediate answers, but we must trust God's timing. When the time is right, He will show us the full picture.

Think about how a parent walks with a toddler. When

your child is just learning to walk, you don't rush them or pull them along at your speed. You slow down to match their tiny steps. That's how God walks with us. He could move so fast that we'd never keep up, but instead, He slows His pace to match ours, patiently walking beside us as we grow.

It's important to remember that everyone grows at different rates spiritually. **1 Corinthians 3:2 (KJV) says, *"I have fed you with milk, and not with meat: for hitherto ye were not able to bear it, neither yet now are ye able."*** Just as you don't feed a newborn a steak, you don't expect new believers to grasp deep spiritual truths right away. God knows this and will walk with us at our pace, leading us step by step until we are mature enough to press forward, as Paul said, ***"I press toward the mark for the prize of the high calling of God in Christ Jesus."* (Philippians 3:14, KJV).**

However, growth takes time and consistency. It's difficult to help someone grow spiritually when they only engage occasionally, like a student who misses most of their classes. Regular time with God is essential for growth, and the Holy Spirit is our personal tutor, walking with us every day, guiding us at our own pace. **John 14:26 (KJV)** promises, ***"But the Comforter, which is the Holy Ghost, whom the Father will send in my name, he shall teach you all things."*** He is there to help us learn and grow, whether we are crawling, walking, or running in our faith.

But the first step in this journey is a decision. We must decide in our hearts that we want to walk with God, no matter how slow or fast the journey may be. It's a commitment to trust Him, savoring each step as we grow in our understanding of Him.

In conclusion, walking with God is about embracing the journey at His pace. Just as we wouldn't rush through a meal, we shouldn't rush our spiritual growth. Every step, every revelation, is a part of the process, and with the Holy Spirit as our guide, we can trust that we will grow and mature in God's perfect timing. Take each step with Him, savoring the journey, and let God reveal His wisdom in due time.

# **"Repentance: Turning to Walk with God"**

Repentance is much more than just feeling sorry for our sins; it's about making a conscious decision to change direction. It's saying, *"God, I've been walking with the world, following my flesh, and straying toward the systems of this world, but now I choose to walk with You."* Repentance is a decision to leave behind what pulls us away from God and begin walking step by step with Him. As **Psalm 23:1-4 (KJV)** reminds us, *"The LORD is my shepherd; I shall not want... Yea, though I walk through the valley of the shadow of death, I will fear no evil: for thou art with me; thy rod and thy staff they comfort me."* Even when we face the darkest valleys, God is with us, guiding us as our Shepherd.

However, the key question isn't whether God will walk with us, but whether we will choose to walk with Him. Just as a shepherd leads the sheep, so God leads us, but we must be willing to follow. In my family, I often tell my children, *"Keep up with me! Walk with me!"* As the head of the household, I set the direction, and they follow. Similarly, in our spiritual walk, we don't tell God where to go; we follow His lead. **John 10:27 (KJV)** says, *"**My sheep hear my voice, and I know them, and they follow me.**"*

It's important to understand that God isn't following us—He is leading, and we must follow His path. Sheep follow the shepherd, but goats are different. Goats are independent, stubborn, and follow whatever their appetite desires. I've had both goats and sheep, and I've seen the difference firsthand. Goats will eat anything, even trash, while sheep are more selective in their diet. This is a fitting metaphor for spiritual life: sheep follow the Shepherd and stay on the right path, but goats will wander, eating anything they come across. **Philippians 3:19 (KJV)** describes those who are led by their flesh, saying, *"**Whose end is destruction, whose God is their belly, and whose glory is in their shame, who mind earthly things.**"*

Many people in the church today may think they are following God, but in reality, they are following their own desires, like goats who eat whatever is in front of them. As we are told in **Matthew 25:32-33 (KJV),** at the end of time, Jesus will separate the sheep from the goats. The goats, having refused to follow the Shepherd, will face a different destiny than the sheep who followed

Him.

Walking with God is an everyday decision. It's not just about walking on the mountaintops but also through the valleys. We will stumble at times, and there will be moments when we are led astray by seducing spirits. But when we fall, we must get back up. **Proverbs 24:16 (KJV)** encourages us, *"For a just man falleth seven times, and riseth up again."* Even if we stray, we must always return to the Shepherd's path, knowing that His grace is there to guide us back.

In today's world, many will try to convince you that it doesn't matter how you live or what choices you make—that God doesn't care about your walk. But **Deuteronomy 10:12 (KJV)** says otherwise: *"And now, Israel, what doth the LORD thy God require of thee, but to fear the LORD thy God, to walk in all his ways, and to love him, and to serve the LORD thy God with all thy heart and with all thy soul."* Walking with God is a consistent theme throughout the Bible, and it's a daily choice to live according to His will.

In conclusion, repentance is the first step in turning away from the ways of the world and deciding to walk with God. As sheep follow their shepherd, so must we follow Jesus, making the choice every day to stay on the path He has set before us. When we walk with God, we walk in His grace, His protection, and His love, knowing that no matter where the journey takes us, He is always with us.

# **"Walking in the Light: A Journey with God"**

Before we come to know Christ, we walk according to the ways of the world. **Ephesians 2:2-3 (KJV)** says, ***"Wherein in time past ye walked according to the course of this world, according to the prince of the power of the air, the spirit that now worketh in the children of disobedience."*** Our conversations, actions, and even our dress reflected the world because we were one with it. We followed the same path as the world because we were lost in its ways.

But now, having been washed in the blood of Christ and born again, we are called to a different walk. **Ephesians 2:10 (KJV) tells us, *"For we are his workmanship, created in Christ Jesus unto good works, which God hath before ordained that we should walk in them."*** This new walk is not in our old ways but in the good works that God has prepared for us. Walking with God is a daily journey, a step-by-step progression of faith and obedience.

Noah serves as a powerful example. **Genesis 6:9 (KJV)** says, ***"Noah was a just man and perfect in his generations, and Noah walked with God."*** Because Noah walked with God, he found grace and was rescued from the flood that wiped out the earth. This principle still holds true today—only those who walk with God will be saved. The world may be filled with violence and corruption, just as in Noah's time, but those who stay close to God will find safety in His presence.

We must reflect deeply on this: Are we truly walking with God, or are we merely walking alongside the world, trying to please others? **Galatians 1:10 (KJV)** reminds us, *"For if I yet pleased men, I should not be the servant of Christ."* Walking with God means setting aside the need to please others and focusing solely on where God is leading us.

Ask yourself, *"Am I walking with God?"* It's a question of great importance because where your feet are, your heart is also. **Luke 12:34 (KJV)** says, *"For where your treasure is, there will your heart be also."* If your treasure is in the things of this world, that's where your heart and feet will be, but if your treasure is in the Lord, you will walk closely with Him.

Walking with God is a pilgrimage, a journey. Sometimes we stumble, we miss the mark, or we stray from the path. But when we get lost, God finds us and brings us back. As the hymn declares, *"I once was lost, but now am found, was blind, but now I see."* When we were walking with the world, holding hands with sin, we were lost. But now, through Christ, we have been found, and He leads us on the path of righteousness.

**1 John 1:7 (KJV)** says, *"But if we walk in the light, as he is in the light, we have fellowship one with another, and the blood of Jesus Christ his Son cleanseth us from all sin."* Walking with God means walking in the light, in truth and action, not just in words. As **1 John 3:18 (KJV)** reminds us, *"My little children,

**let us not love in word, neither in tongue; but in deed and in truth."*** True faith is shown by how we walk, not just what we say.

There's only one path to heaven, and it's through Jesus Christ. **John 14:6 (KJV) says, *"I am the way, the truth, and the life: no man cometh unto the Father, but by me."*** The world may claim there are many paths, but we know there is only one Shepherd, one name under heaven by which we are saved.

In conclusion, walking with God is not just a momentary decision—it's a lifelong journey. It's about leaving behind the ways of the world and choosing to walk in the light of Christ, step by step. There is only one way to heaven, and that is through Jesus. Let us walk with Him, not just in words but in truth and action, trusting Him to lead us home.

# **"Walking with God: Trusting the Path to Miracles"**

In today's world, we face many false prophets who claim that it doesn't matter which path you walk, and that in the end, we'll all reach the same destination. But the Bible tells us that this is a lie. There is a straight and narrow path, a high and holy way, and we are called to walk it with God. Jesus said in **Matthew 7:14 (KJV), *"Because strait is the gate, and narrow is the way, which leadeth unto life, and few there be that find it."***

We can't focus on the mountains that lie ahead, the valleys we may pass through, or the rivers we must cross. Our concern is to stay close to God, step by step, trusting Him to guide us. As we walk with Him, the fruit of our lives will show if we're truly on the right path. Jesus said in **Matthew 7:16 (KJV), *"Ye shall know them by their fruits."*** So, how do we know if we're walking with God? It's revealed by the fruit in our lives—love, joy, peace, patience, kindness, goodness, faithfulness, gentleness, and self-control **(Galatians 5:22-23, KJV).**

Looking at how others are walking can often trip us up. We cannot force anyone to walk with God. Each of us has our own journey, and we must stay focused on our own walk. Noah walked with God, and God spoke directly to him, warning him of the coming flood **(Genesis 6:9, KJV).** Noah tried to warn others, but they did not listen. In the same way, those who walk with God today will warn others of the dangers ahead, urging them to repent and follow the Lord. The true gospel is always about the goodness and severity of God.

In the days of Jeremiah, Israel was blessed, yet they turned away from God. Jeremiah faithfully warned them for forty years, but few heeded his words. As **Deuteronomy 10:12 (KJV)** says, ***"And now, Israel, what doth the LORD thy God require of thee, but to fear the LORD thy God, to walk in all his ways, and to love him, and to serve the LORD thy God with all thy heart and with all thy soul."*** Walking with God means obeying His commands and trusting in His wisdom, even when we don't understand the full plan.

Sometimes, I feel that these messages are more for me than anyone else. I'm not preaching at you—I'm preaching to myself. **Philippians 2:12 (KJV) tells us to *"work out your own salvation with fear and trembling."*** In the same way, we must walk out our own salvation, day by day, with a humble heart. As it was in the days of Noah, very few people are truly walking with God today. If we were to go back in time, I imagine we'd find countless false prophets telling people it didn't matter how they lived because God's love would cover everything.

Yet the true prophets, like Jeremiah, spoke the hard truth. Jeremiah prophesied for forty years, warning the people, but they ignored him. Similarly, God appeared to Abraham and said, *"**Walk with me**"* **(Genesis 17:1, KJV).** When Abraham asked where they were going, God didn't give him all the details. Abraham had to trust that God knew best, even when the future was unclear.

Walking with God often means giving up things we don't understand and trusting Him completely. **Proverbs 3:5-6 (KJV) tells us, *"Trust in the LORD with all thine heart; and lean not unto thine own understanding. In all thy ways acknowledge him, and he shall direct thy paths."*** When God calls us to give something up or take a step of faith, we must simply obey and walk with Him, trusting that He knows what's best.

It's in these moments of complete surrender that miracles happen. When we stop trying to figure everything out and simply trust in God's leading, we open the door for

Him to work wonders in our lives. Walking with God doesn't require a lot of thinking—just faith.

In conclusion, walking with God is about trusting Him completely, even when we don't know where the journey will lead. It's about staying close to Him and obeying His voice, one step at a time. Miracles happen when we let go of our need to understand and lean fully on His wisdom. Let us walk with God in faith, knowing that He will guide us on the path to life.

# Stabbed in the Face Multiple Times by a Demon-Possessed Woman

After arriving in Anchorage, Alaska, I felt prompted by the Holy Spirit to stop by a small full gospel church I used to visit, called The Neighborhood Full Gospel Church. By divine timing, I ran into an evangelist I had known during my time in the Navy on Adak Island. We reminisced about our experiences in Adak, and he shared how the Lord had placed on his heart the mission of starting an evangelistic outreach center in Mount Union, Pennsylvania. He invited me to join him and his wife to help establish the ministry. I agreed, planning to fly back to Wisconsin, where they would pick me up. However, before leaving Alaska, God had one more assignment for me—a precious but demon-possessed woman needed to be set free.

One Sunday, we decided to attend a small, rustic church

along the road to Fairbanks. I was the first to enter the church, and immediately I noticed an elderly woman sitting alone in the pews. The moment our eyes met, I felt an intense demonic presence in her. Without warning, she jumped up and ran out of the church. Right then, I knew God was leading me to help her.

After the service, I asked the pastor about the woman. He told me she wasn't a member of the church but would come in occasionally. He mentioned she lived with her husband in a run-down house off a dirt road. I asked if it would be okay to visit her, and the pastor had no problem with it, especially since she wasn't a regular part of his congregation.

Following the pastor's directions, we arrived at a house that looked exactly as described—run-down, with a yard overflowing with junk. It reminded me of the TV show *Sanford and Son,* but with ten times more clutter. As we got out of the car, her husband greeted us, thanking God for sending us to help his tormented wife. He explained she was in the kitchen.

As we approached the house, we navigated through the cluttered yard and entered their summer kitchen. There, we saw his wife standing at a large utility sink, peeling carrots with a large butcher's knife. As I spoke to her about Jesus, she slowly turned her head, and what I saw next was terrifying. Her head turned without her body moving, and her eyes were glowing red. It felt like I was in a horror movie.

Fear gripped my heart, but I immediately countered it by

quoting Scripture: *"**For God hath not given us the spirit of fear; but of power, and of love, and of a sound mind**"* (2 Timothy 1:7, KJV). I continued sharing about Jesus, but before I knew it, she lunged at me with the knife in hand. Leaping through the air, she wrapped her legs around my waist and began striking my face with the knife. I felt the impact but didn't realize at the time that she was using the knife.

In the heat of the attack, I declared, **"In the Name of Jesus!"** The moment those words left my mouth, she was ripped off of me by an invisible force and thrown across the room, slamming into the wall. Despite the impact, she wasn't hurt. I continued to cast the demons out of her in the Name of Jesus, and soon, she was completely delivered, finally free from the torment that had plagued her for decades.

Once she was in her right mind, I asked her how she had become possessed. Tearfully, she told me her story. When she was a young girl, her uncle had molested and raped her. After he passed away, his spirit began visiting her at night, continuing to molest her for over fifty years. She didn't know it was a familiar spirit, a demonic force disguised as her uncle, tormenting her night after night. That day, she gave her heart to Jesus, and a beautiful peace came over her, completely transforming her countenance. She and her husband began attending church with us until I left Alaska.

Years later, the evangelist who had been with me that day heard me recounting the story. After the service, he approached me to clarify a critical detail. I had thought the woman was merely hitting me with her hand, but he had seen the whole thing from behind. He revealed that she had been stabbing me in the face with the large butcher knife, yet I had not been harmed. Not a single mark was left on my skin. He had expected to see blood pouring from my face, but God had miraculously protected me from the knife.

I am fully convinced that if I had not been walking in holiness and obedience to God, the demon in that woman would have succeeded in killing me. Many in the body of Christ try to deal with demonic powers while living outside of God's will. But when we walk in the Holy Spirit, in obedience, and in absolute love for Jesus, no power in hell can harm us.

As **Daniel 6:22** says, ***"My God hath sent his angel, and hath shut the lions' mouths, that they have not hurt me: forasmuch as before him innocence was found in me."*** That day, God's divine protection was my shield, just as He promises to those who walk in faith and obedience to Him.

# CHAPTER EIGHT
# **"Eyes on Jesus: Walking the Path of Faith"**

Walking with God doesn't require a high IQ or extensive thinking—it simply takes faith, trust, and love. Just like when you walk hand-in-hand with someone you love, your eyes are only on them. You're not worried about where your feet are going because your focus is on that person. This is how God wants us to walk with Him, with our eyes fixed on Jesus, as **Hebrews 12:2 (KJV)** reminds us: *"**Looking unto Jesus the author and finisher of our faith."***

When we are truly walking with God, the world can't relate to us. Our path is different, our destination is different. We may say, *"I don't do that anymore because I'm walking with a new partner."* Yes, we still dance, but now it's with the Holy Spirit. We still drink, but now we drink of the living water that Jesus gives **(John 4:14, KJV)**. Our focus has shifted, and we are walking toward heaven, not the things of this world.

**Deuteronomy 11:21 (KJV)** speaks of God's desire for His people: *"That your days may be multiplied, and the days of your children, in the land which the LORD sware unto your fathers to give them, as the days of heaven upon the earth."* God wants to give us a taste of heaven right here on earth when we walk with Him.

In **Deuteronomy 10:12 (KJV),** the question is asked: *"And now, Israel, what doth the LORD thy God require of thee, but to fear the LORD thy God, to walk in all his ways, and to love him, and to serve the LORD thy God with all thy heart and with all thy soul?"* Walking with God isn't about knowing every step of the journey ahead—it's about taking each step toward heaven with faith, knowing He's guiding us.

Every decision, every thought, every word we speak is either taking us closer to heaven or closer to hell. This is why the world often thinks we're crazy—they can't understand the path we're on. They're walking toward worldly goals, while we're walking toward eternal life. But double-mindedness can lead us into a rut, and if we stay in that rut, it can become a ditch, and if we remain in that ditch, it becomes a grave. **James 1:8 (KJV)** warns us, *"A double minded man is unstable in all his ways."* Walking with God requires steadfastness and trust, not wavering back and forth.

God, however, is not double-minded. He doesn't change His mind or purpose. **Malachi 3:6 (KJV)** says, *"For I am the LORD, I change not."* From the beginning, God's desire was to create someone who would walk with Him forever. That's His plan for humanity, and it hasn't changed. We must make up our minds to walk with Him, no matter what we face. Even if there are no cattle in the stall or no fruit on the vine, as Job said, *"**Though he slay me, yet will I trust in him**"* **(Job 13:15, KJV).** Our resolve should be to keep walking with God.

There will be times when walking with God offends others, just as it did when Jesus told the 70 disciples to *"**eat my flesh, and drink my blood**"* **(John 6:53, KJV).** Many of them were offended and walked away. Jesus didn't beg them to stay. He turned to His twelve and asked, *"**Will ye also go away?**"* **(John 6:67, KJV).** God doesn't beg us to walk with Him—He invites us, but it's up to us to choose to keep walking, even when it's hard to understand or when the world walks away.

In conclusion, walking with God isn't about understanding every step or knowing every turn. It's about keeping our eyes on Jesus, trusting in His plan, and following Him with a steadfast heart. Whether we face valleys, mountains, or rivers, we know that each step taken with God brings us closer to His eternal kingdom. We must walk with Him, not out of duty, but out of love, trusting Him to guide us every day.

## **"Choosing Jesus: Walking in Truth and Repentance"**

Walking with God requires more than just saying we

follow Him—it requires a deep, unwavering commitment. God doesn't have an inferiority complex. He doesn't need our affirmations or our praise. We are the ones who need Him, and only Jesus can give us what we truly need. As **John 14:6 (KJV)** declares, *"I am the way, the truth, and the life: no man cometh unto the Father, but by me."* Only Jesus can lead us to the truth, and without Him, we are lost.

I've come to learn that no one can do for me what Jesus can. As the old song goes, *"Ain't nobody do me like Jesus."* Yes, I love my family deeply, but if I ever have to choose between them and Jesus, I choose Jesus every time. I've made that decision many times throughout my life. **Matthew 10:37 (KJV)** makes it clear: *"He that loveth father or mother more than me is not worthy of me."* If I must choose between financial security, popularity, or Jesus, I will always choose Jesus.

I could preach feel-good sermons that would make everyone in the room feel proud and comfortable. I could make you so happy that you'd kiss my feet and pour your money into buckets. But I won't. I dare not. I refuse to tell you that you are walking with God if you're truly walking with the devil. I won't pretend you're headed for heaven when your actions prove otherwise. **Matthew 7:21 (KJV)** warns us, *"Not every one that saith unto me, Lord, Lord, shall enter into the kingdom of heaven; but he that doeth the will of my Father which is in heaven."*

I'm here to tell you the truth because I love you and because I know that without Christ, we are all lost. I have chosen to walk with God, and I invite you to do the same. But understand this—few will truly walk with God in these last days. Many will say they are walking with Him, but their lives will tell a different story. The Pharisees thought they were walking with God, but they weren't. Their hearts were far from Him, as Jesus said in **Matthew 15:8 (KJV)**, *"**This people draweth nigh unto me with their mouth, and honoureth me with their lips; but their heart is far from me."**

We must be careful not to deceive ourselves. **Deuteronomy 10:12 (KJV)** lays it out plainly: *"**And now, Israel, what doth the LORD thy God require of thee, but to fear the LORD thy God, to walk in all his ways, and to love him, and to serve the LORD thy God with all thy heart and with all thy soul."*** Walking with God isn't just a casual stroll; it's a lifelong commitment to follow Him with all our heart and soul, every day.

Even the apostles weren't immune to straying. In Galatians 2, Peter began walking in a way that wasn't right, and Paul had to confront him. **Galatians 2:14 (KJV)** says, *"**But when I saw that they walked not uprightly according to the truth of the gospel, I said unto Peter before them all…"*** Peter had to repent, and thank God, he did. Repentance is essential. It's acknowledging that we've gone astray and turning back to God. It's a vital part of walking with Him.

So many people think they are walking with God, but if they examined their lives honestly, they might find that they are not. **Psalm 1:1 (KJV)** tells us, *"**Blessed is the man that walketh not in the counsel of the ungodly."* Are we letting the ungodly influence us, or are we truly walking with God? It's a question we must all ask ourselves.

In conclusion, walking with God is not just about saying the right words—it's about living in truth and repentance. It's about making hard choices, even when they cost us dearly. But in choosing Jesus, we choose life, truth, and eternal fellowship with God. Let's commit to walking with Him, not just in word, but in heart, soul, and deed.

---

# **"Walking with God: A Journey of Faith and Commitment"**

**\*"Blessed is the man that walketh not in the counsel of the ungodly, nor standeth in the way of sinners, nor sitteth in the seat of the scornful. But his delight is in the law of the Lord; and in his law doth he meditate day and night."\* (Psalm 1:1-2, KJV).** This scripture beautifully encapsulates the life of one who chooses to walk with God. It speaks of a life grounded in the Word, one that avoids the distractions and pitfalls of the ungodly.

Walking with God is the greatest purpose we can have in life. We were created for this very reason. We weren't made just to exist or to chase after fleeting worldly pleasures. No, we were made to walk in close companionship with our Creator. **Genesis 3:8 (KJV)** describes God walking in the garden in the cool of the day, calling out to Adam and Eve. This illustrates His desire for relationship and communion with us.

Angels, though mighty and magnificent, were not made to be God's companions in the same way. Nor were animals, despite their beauty and significance in creation. God made us—human beings—in His image to walk with Him. Every aspect of creation is a reflection of His goodness and creativity, but our purpose goes deeper. We were designed to walk with God, to be in a close and loving relationship with Him.

However, in this world, we face many obstacles that try to hinder our walk with God. We live in a time where distractions abound, and it's easy to get entangled in the cares of life. **Hebrews 12:1 (KJV)** calls us to *"**lay aside every weight, and the sin which doth so easily beset us, and let us run with patience the race that is set before us."*** Just as a runner strips away unnecessary weight to run more efficiently, we must let go of the things that slow us down in our walk with God.

We are warned in **Matthew 24:12 (KJV),** *"**And because iniquity shall abound, the love of many shall wax cold."*** Many who once walked closely with God will turn away. They'll stop walking in the Spirit and begin walking in the flesh. But **Galatians 5:16 (KJV)** gives us a clear direction: *"**This I say then, Walk in the Spirit, and ye shall not fulfil the lust of the flesh."*** When we choose to walk with God, we won't give in to the desires of the flesh. The Spirit will guide us.

It's important to remember that this is a message for

believers. Sinners don't wrestle with walking in the Spirit because they aren't trying to do what's right in the first place. But for those of us who are born again, walking with God can sometimes feel like a tug of war between the Spirit and the flesh. This is where true misery sets in—not for the sinner, but for the Christian who tries to walk in two different directions. As Jesus said in **Matthew 6:24 (KJV), *"No man can serve two masters."***

Trying to live both ways, half in the world and half in the Spirit, will tear you apart. You can't walk with God while also walking in the flesh. **James 1:8 (KJV)** warns, ***"A double minded man is unstable in all his ways."*** You'll feel miserable, conflicted, and out of peace. And in that misery, it becomes difficult to win others to Christ. If you're unhappy and divided in your walk, how can you lead your family or loved ones to the joy of the Lord?

The most critical decision we must make is to fully commit to walking with God. We can't afford to let the things of this world distract us or split our loyalty. As **1 John 2:15 (KJV)** says, ***"Love not the world, neither the things that are in the world. If any man love the world, the love of the Father is not in him."*** We must choose to walk with God with our whole hearts, not half-heartedly.

In conclusion, walking with God is not a part-time commitment or a divided effort. It's a journey of faith, one that requires us to let go of the things that hold us back and focus entirely on Him. As we walk with God, we find peace, joy, and fulfillment that the world could never offer. Let us choose to walk in the Spirit, and not in the flesh, so that we can truly live out the purpose for which we were created.

# **"Walking in the Spirit: A Life of Faith and Separation"**

There are many churches today that won't challenge you to live a holy life, to walk in the Spirit, or to turn away from sin. In some places, they tolerate covetousness, immorality, and even indulge in worldly amusements showing secular movies at the church for family nights. But as a follower of Christ, you have to decide—who will you walk with? The truth is, you can do whatever you want outside the church building, and that's none of my business. I'm not a preacher who digs up the sins of others. The Bible says in **Proverbs 16:27 (KJV), *"An ungodly man diggeth up evil."*** So when I hear rumors or see others fall, I don't dig for more information. Instead, my heart breaks, and I pray for them. That's walking in love.

I've learned that we must walk with God and not let anything stop us from doing so. **Galatians 5:18 (KJV)** says, ***"But if ye be led of the Spirit, ye are not under the law."*** However, the minute we stop walking in the Spirit, we place ourselves under the law again, under the law of sin and death. When you walk in the flesh, the curse of the law becomes active in your life evn if you have believed on Christ. But **Galatians 3:13 (KJV)** reminds us, *"**Christ hath redeemed us from the curse of the law.**"* He did this so that we could walk in the Spirit, free from the curse.

In **Galatians 6:7-8 (KJV)**, Paul gives a sober warning: *"**Be not deceived; God is not mocked: for whatsoever a man soweth, that shall he also reap. For he that soweth to his flesh shall of the flesh reap corruption; but he that soweth to the Spirit shall of the Spirit reap life everlasting.**"* Walking in the Spirit means reaping the fruit of the Spirit—love, joy, peace, patience, gentleness, goodness, faith, meekness, and self-control **(Galatians 5:22-23, KJV)**. If you're walking with God, you're walking in these things. But if you walk in the flesh, you will reap death—spiritual separation from God.

Before I was born again, I never walked in the Spirit. I didn't know what it meant to walk in love, joy, or peace. But since I accepted Christ, I've learned to walk in those ways. Still, I have to choose daily to keep walking with God and not to fall back into walking with the world. The Bible is clear: *"**Ye cannot drink the cup of the Lord, and the cup of devils**"* **(1 Corinthians 10:21, KJV)**. There must be a separation. You cannot serve God and mammon **(Matthew 6:24, KJV)**.

Throughout scripture, we see examples of men and women who had to make a choice to walk with God no matter the cost. Daniel, Shadrach, Meshach, and Abednego were willing to face death rather than bow to

**idols (Daniel 3:16-18, KJV).** They had made up their hearts and minds—they would walk with God, even if it meant being thrown into the fiery furnace. And God delivered them.

In my own life, I've faced situations where my faith was tested. I once returned to Chicago to preach to a gang that had threatened to kill me if I didn't stop. I told them, *"**Do what you have to do, but I won't stop walking with God."*** And thank God, they couldn't kill me. That's what it means to walk in the Spirit—you stay faithful, even in the face of danger or persecution.

In conclusion, walking in the Spirit means living a life of faith, separated from the world, and fully committed to God. We must be willing to stand firm, even when the world pressures us to compromise. Whether we face ridicule, persecution, or temptation, we can be confident that walking with God is the only path that leads to life and peace.

# ** "Walking with God: A Call to a Higher Walk of Faith"**

There comes a time in every believer's life when you must decide who you will walk with. Many today are deceived, walking with the world, convinced by false prophets that they can live any way they want and still make it to heaven. This is a lie. The Bible tells us in **Matthew 7:14 (KJV), *"Because strait is the gate, and narrow is the way, which leadeth unto life, and few**

**there be that find it."\*** The path to God is narrow, and it requires a life separated from the ways of the world.

In the days of Jeremiah, the prophet cried out for 40 years, pleading with the people to return to the commandments of God, to walk with Him, and to live in obedience. But they would not listen. They continued to walk in rebellion, and eventually, destruction came upon them. The book of **Lamentations 1:12 (KJV)** records Jeremiah's heartbreak as he witnessed the devastation: **\*"Is it nothing to you, all ye that pass by? behold, and see if there be any sorrow like unto my sorrow."\***

God has always desired that we walk with Him. It is a privilege to walk with the Creator of the universe, but many ignore this call. Imagine if a renowned statesman or successful figure called you and asked to spend a day with you. You would drop everything for the chance to walk with them. But how much greater is it that God Himself—the Almighty—calls us daily to walk with Him? He's calling us to walk through our problems, difficulties, and trials. He promises to walk us out of our sickness and through our mental torment, bringing healing to every area of our lives.

In **Genesis 5:24 (KJV)**, it says, **\*"And Enoch walked with God: and he was not; for God took him."\*** Enoch's walk with God was so intimate that God took him to be with Him. Enoch wasn't focused on wealth, fame, or the pleasures of this world. He simply desired to walk with God. Today, God is offering you that same opportunity—to walk with Him, to live in His presence, and to experience His love, peace, and guidance.

Walking with God requires a decision. It means separating yourself from the things that hinder your relationship with Him. **Hebrews 12:1 (KJV)** says, *****"Let us lay aside every weight, and the sin which doth so easily beset us, and let us run with patience the race that is set before us."***** There are weights and sins that can easily entangle us, but we must choose to lay them aside in order to walk closely with God.

Many people today are running toward destruction, unaware of the eternal consequences of their choices. They are like those in the days of Noah, who ignored the warnings and continued in their sinful ways until the flood came. In **Matthew 24:37-39 (KJV),** Jesus said, *****"But as the days of Noe were, so shall also the coming of the Son of man be."***** Just like in Noah's time, many today are too distracted to hear the call to walk with God.

As believers, we must be careful who we choose to walk with. Birds of a feather flock together. If we are not walking with God, we cannot lead others to Him. If we walk with those who live in rebellion against God, we are in danger of following them into destruction. **Amos 3:3 (KJV) says, *****"Can two walk together, except they be agreed?"***** Who are you walking with today?

Walking with God means walking in His Spirit. **Galatians 5:16 (KJV)** says, *****"This I say then, Walk in the Spirit, and ye shall not fulfil the lust of the flesh."***** When we walk in the Spirit, we bear the fruit of the Spirit—love, joy, peace, patience, kindness, goodness, faithfulness, gentleness, and self-control **(Galatians 5:22-23, KJV)**. Walking with God transforms our lives and brings us closer to His heart.

In conclusion, walking with God is the greatest privilege we can ever have. It requires dedication, separation from the world, and a heart fully surrendered to Him. If we choose to walk with Him, we will experience His love, peace, and presence in ways that we never thought possible. Let's commit today to walking with God—every step, every moment, every day

# Anointed to Flip Hamburgers

Kathleen and I were married on August 19, 1978. Three days after our wedding, we set off for Broken Arrow, Oklahoma, to attend Bible school together. When we got married, I didn't have a penny to my name, and Kathleen had to purchase our wedding bands herself. Not only that, but she lost the financial support she had been receiving from her deceased father's social security, which ended when she married. Her father had died in a tragic car accident when she was six years old, and now, without any source of income, we found ourselves facing new challenges. I also had to pay off her existing college tuition, making our situation even more difficult.

It took tremendous faith for Kathleen to marry me and head off to Bible school with someone she barely knew, with no money and no natural source of income. When we arrived in Broken Arrow, we both found work at McDonald's to support ourselves. After finishing our

Bible school classes, which ended by noon, we would return to our apartment, change clothes, and head to work.

For over three years, I had been pouring my life into God's will, and I was determined to give Jesus everything I had. No matter what job I took, I committed myself to doing it with all the ability God had given me. This attitude didn't change when I worked at McDonald's. I saw the job as an opportunity to glorify God, even if it was just cleaning tables, toilets, or emptying garbage. My heart was full of gratitude, and I was determined to be the best worker my employer had ever hired.

One day, as Kathleen and I walked into McDonald's, the manager seemed visibly upset. When I asked him what was wrong, he explained that none of his regular cooks had shown up, and the customers were backing up with no one to prepare the food. Without hesitation, I told him I would take care of it. Though I had no experience cooking at McDonald's, I stepped up.

As I headed toward the grill area, I cried out to God in my heart, saying, "Father, in the name of Jesus, I thank You for giving me the ability to do this job. You are my strength and my wisdom. Now, Lord, please supernaturally enable me to do this for Your glory." As soon as I prayed, I felt the quickening of the Holy Spirit in my mind and body.

Though I had observed the cooks in action, I had no detailed knowledge of how to prepare the sandwiches or manage the kitchen. But as I stepped behind the grill, divine knowledge flooded my mind. I knew exactly what to do. The restaurant was crowded, but I entered a zone where time seemed to slow down, and I began moving with supernatural speed.

I grabbed the different meats for the grill, dropped the fish fillets into the deep fryer, and quickly filled baskets with French fries. I worked like a well-oiled machine, making no mistakes and feeling a deep sense of peace. I was enjoying every moment, completely lost in the power of the Holy Ghost as I moved through the kitchen.

At one point, I noticed the manager standing off to the side, staring at me with his mouth hanging open in disbelief. He watched as I prepared Big Macs, Quarter Pounders, fish fillets, and fries with precision. Not once did I falter or miss a step. I never took a break, never got tired, and never felt overwhelmed.

When my shift ended, the manager approached me. "Mike," he said, "how long have you been a cook?" He told me he had never seen anything like it. I explained to him that I had never flipped a hamburger or made a sandwich in my life. He was utterly shocked and asked, "Well, how did you do it?" That's when I shared with him about Jesus Christ, His supernatural life, and how God's divine power works in the hearts of those who trust Him.

As my wife and I left McDonald's that day, I was filled with excitement, eager to see what God had in store for us next. This is how I've lived my life for almost 50 years—moving in faith and trusting in the power of God to accomplish the impossible.

*"I can do all things through Christ which strengtheneth me"* (Philippians 4:13, KJV).

# CHAPTER NINE
## **"God's Design: Walking in His Ways and Understanding His Purpose"**

God declares in **Malachi 3:6 (KJV),** *"For I am the Lord, I change not; therefore ye sons of Jacob are not consumed."* Similarly, **Hebrews 13:8 (KJV)** reminds us that *"Jesus Christ the same yesterday, and today, and forever."* God's ways are higher than ours, and His thoughts are far beyond human understanding. **Isaiah 55:9 (KJV)** tells us, *"For as the heavens are higher than the earth, so are my ways higher than your ways, and my thoughts than your thoughts."* In this world, we often place value on things that are insignificant to God, but we must remember that He made us for His pleasure, for His companionship, and to walk in His ways.

When God looks down on the earth, He sees all of humanity—like a farmer watching his crops or parents looking over their children. He sees people in different stages of life and faith. First, He sees those conceived in their mother's wombs. Even the unborn and the newly born, though they are alive in the natural world, are still alive unto Him. They are innocent, not yet having knowingly or willfully sinned against God. Jesus spoke of the value of children in **Matthew 19:14 (KJV), *"Suffer little children, and forbid them not, to come unto me: for of such is the kingdom of heaven."***

However, as individuals grow, they come to a point of accountability, where they begin to make choices that go against their conscience and, in doing so, murder the nature of God within their hearts. When we knowingly choose sin, we suppress the voice of God inside us. In this sense, every person who reaches this point of awareness becomes a spiritual murderer because they have killed the righteousness of God in their hearts. Yet, this is precisely why Christ came—to redeem murderers like us, to give us life through His death on the cross.

It was our sin that put Him on that cross. Every sin we have committed contributed to His crucifixion. **John 8:44 (KJV)** records Jesus telling the Pharisees, ***"Ye are of your father the devil, and the lusts of your father ye will do. He was a murderer from the beginning, and abode not in the truth, because there is no truth in him."*** Even though the Pharisees did not realize it, their desire to kill Jesus revealed the sinfulness deep within them. The same is true for all of us—if Christ is not reigning in our hearts, evil will manifest itself, and we will act according to the sinful nature. Jesus said in **Matthew 15:19 (KJV), *"For out of the heart proceed evil thoughts, murders, adulteries, fornications, thefts, false witness, blasphemies."***

Our society today seems to be moving closer to that

reality, where the sinful nature of man is more evident. But there is hope in Christ. God sees the state of every person. Some are still spiritually alive unto Him, while others have not yet been born again. And then there are those who have been born again but are still growing in their faith. Jesus illustrated this in the Parable of the Sower **(Matthew 13),** where the seed represents the Word of God, and the condition of the soil represents the hearts of people. Some receive the Word, but the cares of this world choke it out; others endure for a time but fall away when trials come.

The call today is to recognize that God made us for His companionship, for His pleasure. **Revelation 4:11 (KJV)** reminds us, *"**Thou art worthy, O Lord, to receive glory and honour and power: for thou hast created all things, and for thy pleasure they are and were created."*** Walking with God means choosing His ways over the ways of the world, acknowledging that our sins once made us enemies of God, but through Christ, we are brought back into fellowship with Him.

Let us take time to reflect on our walk with God, seeking His guidance, and asking for the strength to lay aside the sins that so easily entangle us **(Hebrews 12:1).**

## ** "Created for Companionship: Walking with God in Eternity"**

In **Mark 4:5-6 (KJV),** Jesus shared the parable of the sower, saying, *"**Some fell on stony ground, where it** had not much earth; and immediately it sprang up, because it had no depth of earth: But when the sun was up, it was scorched; and because it had no root, it withered away."*** This illustrates how those who receive the Word with joy may stumble when faced with persecution, just as shallow roots cannot sustain growth in hard soil. Jesus also speaks of seed that falls among thorns, representing people who hear the Word but allow the cares of this world to choke it out. We must ensure our hearts are fertile ground for God's Word, producing a bountiful harvest for His kingdom—thirtyfold, sixtyfold, or a hundredfold.

In **Revelation 3:16 (KJV),** God addresses the lukewarm state of the Laodicean church, saying, ***"So then because thou art lukewarm, and neither cold nor hot, I will spue thee out of my mouth."*** But God desires us to be "hot" for Him—to be passionate and committed in our walk with Jesus. This kind of fervent devotion is what it means to be on fire for the Lord, continually seeking intimacy with Him.

Why did God create humanity? It wasn't because of our appearance, intelligence, or achievements. He created us for companionship, not out of need, but out of love. Just as parents delight in pouring love and care into their children, God delights in expressing His love to us. He desires to walk with us, to fellowship with us, and to share an intimate relationship with us. In **Genesis 3:8 (KJV),** we read how ***"they heard the voice of the Lord God walking in the garden in the cool of the day."*** This image of God walking with His creation illustrates the closeness He desires with us.

God's plans for us extend beyond this life. In eternity, we will walk with Him. In fact, **Revelation 3:21 (KJV)** reveals His promise: *****"To him that overcometh will I grant to sit with me in my throne, even as I also overcame, and am set down with my Father in his throne."*** Not only will we walk beside Him, but we will also share in His authority, seated on His throne as part of His eternal family.

Imagine heaven. Picture walking hand in hand with God Himself. We won't be standing in the background, trying to catch a glimpse of Him from afar, as if He were a distant celebrity. Instead, we will be right there beside Him, holding His hand, walking in His presence. **John 10:27 (KJV) says,** *****"My sheep hear my voice, and I know them, and they follow me."*** Our journey with God does not end in this life. It continues in eternity, where we will have an intimate and personal relationship with Him.

Heaven is not a place where some are left on the outskirts looking in. Each of us will be walking side by side with our Heavenly Father, with Jesus, and with the Holy Spirit surrounding us. We will be in His immediate presence, enjoying His glory forever.

As we live our lives now, our closeness to God and our faithfulness will shape our role in eternity. While salvation is a gift to all who believe, the levels of authority and responsibility we hold in heaven will reflect how we walked with God in this life. **Matthew 25:21 (KJV) says,** *****"Well done, thou good and faithful** servant: thou hast been faithful over a few things, I will make thee ruler over many things: enter thou into the joy of thy lord."*

The most wonderful truth is that in eternity, we won't be looking from a distance or wondering where we stand. We will walk hand in hand with our Father, knowing His love personally and experiencing His presence fully. What a privilege it is to walk with God now, as a foretaste of the glorious walk we will share with Him in eternity!

## **Walking with God: A Journey of Faith and Obedience**

From the dawn of time in the Garden of Eden to the end of the Book of Revelation, the Bible is filled with God's call to humanity to walk with Him. The journey of walking with God is not just a mere metaphor but a deliberate act of faith, echoing through the lives of the patriarchs and saints of old. This walk is not one of convenience or fleshly desires, but of steadfast obedience and trust, taking steps alongside the Creator, as shown in the lives of Abraham, Isaac, and the many heroes of faith in Hebrews 11.

When God led the Israelites out of Egypt, He chose to walk with them. It was not a hurried or rushed journey; instead, He slowed the pace, tabernacling with His people, reminding them of His constant presence. Similarly, when He called Abraham, He invited him on a walk—one that would last a lifetime. Abraham, in turn, never stopped walking, neither did Isaac nor the generations after. As Abraham's servant described him in **Genesis 24:40, "The Lord, before whom I walk, will send His angel with thee, and prosper thy way."** Walking with God became a defining characteristic of Abraham's life.

Walking in the flesh, however, is easy; it takes no faith to follow the desires of the world. But walking in the spirit, that requires a deep trust in God and His word. **Romans 8:1** tells us, **"There is therefore now no condemnation to them which are in Christ Jesus, who walk not after the flesh, but after the Spirit."** It takes faith to step away from the comforts of the flesh and walk in step with God.

Our memories can serve as spiritual milestones, like revisiting the paths we've already walked. These moments of victory and testimony are a reminder of God's faithfulness in our lives. We don't dwell on the things that pull us away from His will, as **Philippians 3:13** reminds us, **"Forgetting those things which are behind, and reaching forth unto those things which are before,"** but we do reflect on God's goodness. Just as Saul lost his way when he forgot where he came from, we must always remember our humble beginnings and how God has rescued us.

The walk with God is often opposed by the enemy, who desires what he cannot have. From the moment we give our hearts to Christ, the devil seeks to destroy that relationship. It mirrors the way the flesh desires what it should not possess, much like King Ahab coveted Naboth's vineyard **(1 Kings 21).** Yet, the human race belongs to God, and when we begin to walk with Him, all the powers of darkness tremble.

Walking with God is not just a casual stroll; it's an intentional and continuous journey, one that requires us to stay in step with His will. As we see in **Romans 8:1,** those who walk in the Spirit are free from condemnation, and in this freedom, we find the strength to persevere in faith, no matter the opposition.

So, let your fingers walk through the Word, your mind walk through memory lane, and your heart walk with God, trusting that He is with you every step of the way.

## ** Returning to the Father: Walking in the Spirit and Not the Flesh**

**Romans 8:1** declares, **"There is therefore now no condemnation to them which are in Christ Jesus, who walk not after the flesh, but after the Spirit."** This verse brings clarity to the essence of walking with God—living in the Spirit. Many may think that simply being born again means they're walking in the Spirit, but that's not always the case. As I often explain, being in Christ and walking in the Spirit are not automatic.

To walk in the Spirit is to live in fellowship, intimacy, and alignment with God. It's understanding that we are here for His pleasure, as **Revelation 4:11** says, **"Thou**

**art worthy, O Lord, to receive glory and honour and power: for thou hast created all things, and for thy pleasure they are and were created."** Walking with God means seeking to please Him, and living a life that reflects His glory.

But what happens when we walk in the flesh? Scripture tells us in **Romans 8:6, "For to be carnally minded is death; but to be spiritually minded is life and peace."** The moment we shift our focus from the Spirit to the flesh, we place ourselves under the law again. Carnal living pulls us into fear, strife, and bitterness, which are works of the flesh. When you're afraid—whether it's fear of sickness, failure, or hardship—you are walking in the flesh. Yet, the devil doesn't always know when we're in the flesh, for God often shields us in the shadow of His wings.

The story of Job is a prime example. Satan approached God, desiring to attack Job, but God knew Job had been in the flesh, vulnerable to the enemy. Job confessed, **"For the thing which I greatly feared is come upon me" (Job 3:25).** Fear opened a door for the enemy. However, just as God was patient with Job, His grace covers us. Just because we haven't yet faced consequences doesn't mean we are not walking in the flesh—it simply means God's goodness has spared us.

I have encountered many backslidden Christians who admitted that during their time away from God, they were fully aware they'd be lost if they died in their sin. No matter how many preachers claim otherwise, they knew in their hearts that they were far from God. This reflects the story of the prodigal son, who realized his dire condition and said, **"I will arise and go to my father" (Luke 15:18).** When he began walking back to his father, his relationship was restored.

Walking with the Father isn't just a physical act—it's a spiritual journey of faith, intimacy, and obedience. It's when we recognize our distance from Him and return to His embrace that we find true peace. We must come back to our spiritual "Daddy," just like the prodigal son, walking away from the flesh and back into the arms of the Father.

## \*\* Walking in the Spirit: A Journey of Crucifying the Flesh\*\*

In the scriptures, **James 4:8** invites us, **"Draw nigh to God, and he will draw nigh to you."** This is the call for believers to walk in the Spirit and not after the flesh. As **Romans 8:1-2** teaches, those who are in Christ Jesus must seek the things above and set their affections on the heavenly realm, not on earthly desires. **"For ye are dead, and your life is hid with Christ in God" (Colossians 3:3).** Walking in the Spirit involves a continual process of crucifying the flesh, submitting to God's will, and mortifying the sinful desires that seek to pull us away from Him.

Jesus came to condemn sin in the flesh, to eradicate its power over us. Through the law of the Spirit of life in Christ, we are set free from the law of sin and death. The law, though holy, could not bring life because it was weakened through the flesh. **Romans 8:3-4** explains that Christ's sacrifice on the cross achieved what the law could not, for **"what the law could not do, in that it was weak through the flesh, God sending his own Son in the likeness of sinful flesh, and for sin, condemned sin in the flesh."**

The law, including the Ten Commandments, though righteous, could not save us. It is only through Christ's sacrifice and indwelling that we can receive His divine nature. Christ died to live within us, imparting His Spirit and enabling us to live a life of victory over sin. **Galatians 2:20** echoes this truth: **"I am crucified with Christ: nevertheless I live; yet not I, but Christ liveth in me."**

Picture humanity as a vast oyster bed, each soul like an oyster resting at the ocean's bottom. Oysters, much like human hearts, are vulnerable to the world around them. When an irritant, like a grain of sand, gets inside the oyster, it causes pain and distress. But instead of succumbing to the irritation, the oyster responds by covering the foreign object with layers of nacre, eventually forming a pearl. Similarly, God uses the trials and irritants in our lives to produce something precious within us, refining us and making us more like Christ.

The pain and discomfort we experience in the flesh are often opportunities for God's grace to shine through. Just as the oyster turns its pain into a pearl, we are called to transform our struggles into testimonies of God's faithfulness and grace. **Matthew 13:45-46** describes the kingdom of heaven as **"like unto a merchant man, seeking goodly pearls: Who, when he had found one pearl of great price, went and sold all that he had, and bought it."** In the same way, we must be willing to forsake all for the treasure of walking with God, letting Him transform our pain into something beautiful.

In this journey of walking in the Spirit, we fix our eyes on Jesus, who is our life and our strength. By mortifying the deeds of the flesh and seeking the things above, we find life, peace, and true freedom in Christ. Let us continue to draw near to Him, knowing that as we do, He will draw near to us, transforming our hearts and leading us into His glorious presence.

## ** The Pearl of Christ: Overcoming the Flesh and Producing Spiritual Fruit**

**Hebrews 4:12** tells us, **"For the word of God is quick, and powerful, and sharper than any twoedged sword, piercing even to the dividing asunder of soul and spirit, and of the joints and marrow, and is a discerner of the thoughts and intents of the heart."** This verse captures the transformative power of God's word, which pierces through our flesh and plants the seed of Christ within us. Once that seed takes root, our hearts, minds, and thoughts become centered on Jesus. His presence within us grows, much like a pearl within an oyster, until He fills every part of our being.

As we walk with Christ, His life in us enlarges and shines

brighter, transforming us from the inside out. One day, God will open every spiritual "oyster," revealing whether there is a pearl inside—whether the life of Christ has truly been formed within us. As **Matthew 13:45-46** reminds us, **"Again, the kingdom of heaven is like unto a merchant man, seeking goodly pearls: Who, when he had found one pearl of great price, went and sold all that he had, and bought it."** That pearl is Christ in us, the hope of glory.

I recall an experience shared by a fellow pastor who once received an open vision from God regarding his congregation. In this vision, the pastor saw a dark hand with long, sharp fingernails piercing the chests of several people in the congregation. After this demonic hand withdrew, a vacuum was created, and several individuals were sucked out of the church, leaving others to ask, "Where's John? Where's Luanne?" Deeply disturbed, the pastor asked God for understanding. The Lord revealed to him that these individuals were the devil's plants, sent to bring destruction. They offered no resistance because they were not rooted in Christ.

This vision serves as a sobering reminder that not everyone within the church is producing the pearl of Christ. The enemy comes to steal, kill, and destroy **(John 10:10),** and he will target those whose hearts are not fully committed to God. Jesus Himself warned of false believers, the **"tares"** among the **"wheat" (Matthew 13:24-30),** who are sown by the enemy to create division and disruption.

But for those who are truly walking in the Spirit, who are

allowing the life of Christ to be formed within them, there is victory. **Romans 8:3-4** tells us that God sent His Son **"in the likeness of sinful flesh, and for sin, condemned sin in the flesh."** Christ came not just to forgive sin but to destroy its power over us. As 1 John 3:8 declares, "For this purpose the Son of God was manifested, that he might destroy the works of the devil."

Walking in the flesh leads to sin, for it is in the flesh that the devil has power. But when we walk in the Spirit, allowing Christ to live through us, we overcome the flesh and produce the fruit of the Spirit. The goal of our Christian life is to cultivate the pearl of Christ within us, ensuring that we are spiritually fruitful and standing firm against the enemy's schemes.

**Let this be our prayer:** "Lord, produce the pearl of Christ in me. Let Your life grow and enlarge within me so that I may shine with Your glory and stand firm in the face of opposition. Help me to walk in the Spirit and not in the flesh, that Your will may be done in my life." Amen.

## ** Walking in Agreement with God: Fulfilling His Righteousness Through the Spirit**

Throughout the New Testament, the scriptures continue to remind us of the ongoing struggle between walking in the flesh and walking in the Spirit. **Romans 8:4** tells us that Christ condemned sin so **"that the righteousness of the law might be fulfilled in us, who walk not after the flesh, but after the Spirit."** The law was never flawed in itself; it was simply unable to transform us. Yet, through the power of Christ, God promises to write His law on our hearts, allowing us to walk in His ways.

As **Ezekiel 36:27** prophesies, **"And I will put my spirit within you, and cause you to walk in my statutes, and ye shall keep my judgments, and do them."** This is the essence of salvation—God puts His Spirit within us, and we are transformed into doers of the Word, not by our own strength, but by the power of Christ working in us.

I recall an encounter with a Baptist man who argued that we are not saved by works. I explained that it's not about trying to follow a set of rules—it's about Christ living within us. The man asked if I knew the Ten Commandments by heart, and while he couldn't quote them all, he soon realized he was naturally living them out. As the man listed each commandment, I realized, "I'm already doing that!" Without even knowing it, the Spirit of Christ in me was fulfilling the law.

This is the beauty of walking with God—when Christ rules in our hearts, we naturally begin to live according to His Word. **Philippians 2:13** assures us, **"For it is God which worketh in you both to will and to do of his good pleasure."** It is His divine nature within us that enables us to follow His commands, not through legalistic effort, but through His grace and presence in our lives.

Walking with God means agreeing with Him. As **Amos 3:3** asks, **"Can two walk together, except they be agreed?"** So often, we fall into doubt, not agreeing with what God has said. He promises to supply all our needs according to His riches in glory **(Philippians 4:19),** yet how often do we doubt His provision? He calls us to cast all our cares upon Him, because He cares for **us (1 Peter 5:7),** but we hold onto our worries. His Word declares, **"No weapon that is formed against thee shall prosper" (Isaiah 54:17),** yet we allow fear to take root.

To truly walk with God, we must come into agreement with His promises, trusting in His Word and His provision. As we submit ourselves to Him and resist the devil, the enemy will flee **(James 4:7).** Walking in the Spirit is not a passive experience—it requires active agreement with God, trusting that His Word is true and allowing His Spirit to guide us every step of the way.

This is the life Christ calls us to, a life where His Spirit empowers us to fulfill the law of righteousness, not by our efforts, but by His grace. We become doers of the Word because Christ lives in us. The more we agree with what God has said, the more we walk in harmony with Him, fulfilling His purpose and glorifying His name

# Lessons in Spiritual Authenticity from RHEMA

During our time at RHEMA Bible Training College, my wife Kathee and I encountered a diverse array of personalities, as is typical in any Christian organization. Among them was a particular young lady who stood out for her unconventional behaviors, which some might describe as 'flaky.' She had a way of speaking and moving that seemed detached from reality—floating rather than walking, her voice taking on an ethereal quality that didn't seem grounded in reality.

Kathee and I generally kept to ourselves, focusing on our studies and spiritual growth. However, as our time at RHEMA drew to a close, we noticed an increase in grumbling among some of the students. Initially, we listened to some of this, but I felt a strong internal admonition from the Lord to stay out of the fray and focus solely on why we were there: to receive our education and prepare for the mission field.

On graduation day, with our vehicle packed and ready, we left RHEMA immediately after the ceremony, led by a clear directive to move forward into our next phase of ministry without looking back.

Before we departed, an incident occurred that encapsulated my reflections on genuine spirituality. This particular young lady, the one known for her 'floating' demeanor, was walking ahead of Kathee and me one spring day. Without much thought, I simply questioned her aloud, asking why she walked in such an exaggerated manner like she was stepping on clouds. Now I was only 23 years old, and I did not know it would cause an explosion of emotion. She spun around, her demeanor shifting drastically from serene to stormy as she accused me of being carnally minded, and began to give me a tongue lashing.

Her reaction was a stark contrast to the spiritual persona she projected as she floated and spoke like Kathryn Kuhlman. Had she been the serene, spiritual person she claimed, she might have simply smiled and continued on her way. Instead, she lashed out in anger, which suggested to me that her spirituality was not as deep as her outward expressions implied. **James 3:10-18** addresses this discrepancy directly, teaching that true wisdom from above is **"first pure, then peaceable, gentle, and easy to be entreated, full of mercy and good fruits, without partiality, and without hypocrisy."**

This scripture underscores that a person's words and actions should be consistent with the fruits of the Spirit. If someone professes to be spiritual yet exhibits anger, self-righteousness, or an accusative demeanor, it raises questions about the authenticity of their faith.

From that encounter, I learned a valuable lesson about the nature of true spirituality. It's not about outward appearances or mystical affectations but is demonstrated through the fruits of wisdom, peace, and righteousness. As we walked past her and into the building, I decided to leave the situation in God's hands, understanding that it was not my place to judge but to pray for her and focus on my own walk with God. The last I saw of her she was still yelling at me.

In any community, especially a Christian one, you will encounter a range of beliefs and behaviors. It's important to remember that spiritual maturity involves discernment, not just about our own behavior but also understanding and responding appropriately to the behavior of others. If you find yourself attacked or accused by someone who claims to be a follower of Christ, the best response is often to simply walk away and pray for them, entrusting their growth to God. This approach not only preserves peace but also aligns with the divine wisdom that calls us to sow righteousness in peace.

Many years later my daughter questioned me about some times when I preached, I would act and talk a little strange. I told her: Don't blame God or the Holy Spirit if I get over emotional, that's just me not controlling my flesh under the anointing of God!

# CHAPTER TEN
## ** Walking in the Spirit: Renewing the Mind for Life and Peace**

To walk with God, we must first agree with God. As **Romans 8:5** explains, **"For they that are after the flesh do mind the things of the flesh; but they that are after the Spirit the things of the Spirit."** This means that our focus, whether on the things of the flesh or the Spirit, reveals where we are walking. If we are preoccupied with worldly matters, we are walking in the flesh. If our hearts are set on spiritual matters, we are walking in the Spirit.

A great example of this is found in the story of Martha and Mary. In **Luke 10:38-42**, Martha was consumed with the practical tasks of serving, while Mary sat at Jesus' feet, soaking in His words. Martha was in the flesh, focused on duties, but Mary was in the Spirit, focused on Jesus. This doesn't mean that Mary never worked or served—she later anointed Jesus' body for burial **(John 12:3).** The difference lies in priorities; Mary chose to sit at Jesus' feet when it mattered most, while Martha let the cares of the world distract her from the more important moment.

**Romans 8:6** tells us, **"For to be carnally minded is death; but to be spiritually minded is life and peace."** The carnal mind is at odds with God, unable to submit to His law. It's only when we renew our minds that we can align with God's will and walk in the Spirit. **Romans 12:2** instructs us, **"And be not conformed to this world: but be ye transformed by the renewing of your mind, that ye may prove what is that good, and acceptable, and perfect, will of God."**

Renewing the mind is key to spiritual growth. It's a process of immersing ourselves in the Word of God, allowing His truth to replace worldly thinking. Without this renewal, it's impossible to walk in the Spirit. Just as you cannot pass an algebra test without learning basic math, you cannot live a life in the Spirit without preparing your mind with God's Word.

I compare this to studying for a difficult test. Imagine sitting down for a 10th-grade algebra exam when you haven't even mastered basic addition. It would be foolish to expect success without preparation. In the same way, we cannot expect to walk in the Spirit if we haven't renewed our minds and aligned our thoughts with God's truth. **2 Timothy 2:15** encourages us, **"Study to shew thyself approved unto God, a workman that needeth not to be ashamed, rightly dividing the word of truth."**

This process takes effort. Just as someone without a third-grade education must put in the work to learn, we too must invest time and energy into renewing our minds.

It's not legalism—it's a necessary part of growing in Christ. To walk in the Spirit, we must be intentional about feeding our minds with the Word, casting aside the distractions of the flesh, and setting our hearts on things above **(Colossians 3:2).**

In conclusion, if we want to walk in agreement with God, we must actively renew our minds, focusing on His Word and letting it transform us. By doing so, we will walk in the Spirit, experience life and peace, and fulfill the righteousness that God desires for us.

## ** Walking with God: The Path to Faith, Prosperity, and True Understanding**

The difference between walking in the flesh and walking in the Spirit is a recurring theme throughout the New Testament. **Romans 8:8-9** reminds us, **"So then they that are in the flesh cannot please God. But ye are not in the flesh, but in the Spirit, if so be that the Spirit of God dwell in you."** Walking in the flesh leads us away from God because the carnal mind is contrary to His will, making it impossible to please Him without faith **(Hebrews 11:6).** To walk with God, we must agree with Him, even if we don't fully understand everything right away.

I often emphasizes that to begin this journey, we first have to agree with God's Word. If you don't believe a compass is accurate, you'll never trust its direction. Likewise, until you are convinced that the Bible is true and trustworthy, it's impossible to follow God's path. **Romans 12:2** urges us to be **"transformed by the renewing of your mind,"** aligning our thoughts with God's truth.

The essence of walking with God is not just about knowing His Word—it's about spending time with Him. **Deuteronomy 5:33** says, **"Ye shall walk in all the ways which the Lord your God hath commanded you, that ye may live, and that it may be well with you."** God desires us to walk with Him so that we may prosper, be in good health, and bear fruit. As we walk with Him, we begin to understand who He is, just as we get to know someone better the more time we spend with them. **Philippians 3:10** expresses this longing to know Christ intimately: **"That I may know him, and the power of his resurrection."**

Let me share a personal story illustrating the importance of walking with people before entrusting them with responsibility. Many years ago, a ministry called "Jesus is Lord" from Baltimore appeared to be a godsend, offering their expertise at a time when I needed help. However, I made the mistake of not taking the time to walk with them, to truly get to know them. While on vacation, things began to unravel—church property went missing, and when I finally spent time with these individuals, I discovered their hearts were full of strife, bitterness, and resentment. As the Bible says**, "Out of the abundance of the heart the mouth speaketh" (Luke 6:45).** If I had walked with them even for an hour, I would have seen their true nature.

This experience emphasizes the importance of walking with God and spending time with Him. Just as I missed the warning signs because I didn't walk with these individuals, we too can miss God's guidance if we aren't spending enough time with Him. Walking with God isn't just about talking to Him in prayer—it's about listening, aligning our hearts with His, and allowing His Spirit to lead us.

Prayer, isn't powerful in itself. The power lies in Christ. Prayer is simply the connection between us and God, much like an umbilical cord that sustains life. Without Christ, prayer is empty. With Him, it becomes the channel through which we receive strength, guidance, and wisdom.

In conclusion, walking with God is about much more than performing religious duties. It's about agreement with His Word, renewing our minds, and spending intentional time with Him to know Him better. This path leads to spiritual prosperity, health, and a life that pleases God. Let us be mindful of who and what we walk with, ensuring that our steps are always in sync with our Heavenly Father.

## **Walking Worthy of God: Faith, Prayer, and Understanding the Word**

Through nearly 50 years of ministry and countless hours of prayer, I have learned the true nature of walking with God and what it means to be still before Him. Reflecting on those early prayer gatherings—sometimes starting as early as three in the morning and lasting until eight or nine in the evening—I discovered something profound. Those who never grew spiritually were often the ones who did all the talking during prayer, never giving God the space to speak to their hearts. As **Psalm 46:10** says, **"Be still, and know that I am God."**

I found that those who were guilty of something would often talk the most, trying to defend or explain themselves. It's much like how children behave when they've done something wrong—talking non-stop in hopes of covering up their mistake. But just as a parent can see through a child's words, God knows the truth of our hearts. **Deuteronomy 10:12-13** sums it up well: **"And now, Israel, what doth the Lord thy God require of thee, but to fear the Lord thy God, to walk in all his ways, and to love him, and to serve the Lord thy God with all thy heart and with all thy soul."**

Walking with God means walking in a manner worthy of Him, as **1 Thessalonians 2:12** says, **"That ye would walk worthy of God, who hath called you unto his kingdom and glory."** It's not about whether we feel worthy but about choosing to live in a way that reflects God's love and commands. **Colossians 1:10** further emphasizes this: **"That ye might walk worthy of the Lord unto all pleasing, being fruitful in every good work, and increasing in the knowledge of God."**

Walking with God also requires faith. **2 Corinthians 5:7** reminds us, **"For we walk by faith, not by sight."** Faith is what pleases God and connects us to His promises.

Without faith, as **Hebrews 11:6** tells us, it is impossible to please Him.

I recall an encounter with a worship leader who became angry after hearing one of my sermons. The man accused me of preaching legalism and the law. In response, I invited the man to discuss his interpretation of the scripture, particularly the book of Galatians. Having memorized and meditated on the entire book of Galatians many years previously, I could see the bigger picture of what Paul was addressing in his letter. The Judaizers were teaching that salvation required not just faith in Christ but also adherence to the old Jewish laws, like circumcision and keeping the Sabbath.

I explained that I didn't preach circumcision or legalism. Instead, I taught that Christ is our Sabbath, fulfilling the law through His sacrifice. Unfortunately, the conversation grew heated the worship leader yelling at me. The worship leader hung up, called back to apologize, and then hung up again after another round of him yelling. This happened three times before the conversation finally ended. The situation illustrates how misunderstanding or limited knowledge of scripture can lead to frustration and division.

This story serves as a reminder of the importance of fully understanding the Word of God. Pastor Mike's experience shows that it's not enough to simply know bits and pieces of scripture. True wisdom comes from meditating on the whole counsel of God and allowing the Spirit to reveal the deeper truths. As believers, we are called to walk worthy of God, to walk in faith, and to let our understanding of His Word shape our lives.

To walk worthy of the Lord is to be fruitful, to grow in knowledge, and to live in faith. This requires time spent in God's presence—listening, learning, and letting Him guide our steps. As we renew our minds in the Word and walk by faith, we become more aligned with God's will, and our lives begin to reflect His glory.

## ** Walking in the Spirit: Living in Love, Joy, and Liberty**

In his journey of studying and teaching the Word, Pastor Mike emphasizes the importance of understanding the full picture of scripture. When we examine the whole counsel of God, we see the deeper meaning behind Paul's teachings in Galatians. Paul calls believers to **"stand fast therefore in the liberty wherewith Christ hath made us free, and be not entangled again with the yoke of bondage" (Galatians 5:1).** This liberty is not just freedom from the law of circumcision or religious rituals; it's the freedom to walk in the Spirit.

Having begun this journey in the Spirit—walking in God's love, joy, and peace—Paul warns the Galatians against returning to the flesh. He asks them, **"Are ye so foolish? Having begun in the Spirit, are ye now made perfect by the flesh?" (Galatians 3:3).** To walk in the Spirit is to live in God's divine nature, and this means walking in love that **"covers a multitude of sins" (1 Peter 4:8).** It means experiencing joy unspeakable and full of glory **(1 Peter 1:8)** and having peace that surpasses all understanding **(Philippians 4:7)**. These are not fleeting emotions, but deep, abiding realities that come from walking with God.

In contrast, returning to the flesh—to legalistic practices like circumcision, feast days, and observances—leads to division and strife. Paul observed that when believers began focusing on these external rituals, they started devouring one another, arguing over who was more righteous based on outward practices. **Galatians 5:15** warns, **"But if ye bite and devour one another, take heed that ye be not consumed one of another."** This is the outcome of walking in the flesh—strife, envy, and discord.

However, when we walk in the Spirit, we fulfill the law of liberty through love. As Paul writes in **Galatians 5:14, "For all the law is fulfilled in one word, even in this; Thou shalt love thy neighbour as thyself."** Walking in the Spirit produces the fruit of the Spirit: love, joy, peace, long-suffering, gentleness, goodness, faith, meekness, and temperance **(Galatians 5:22-23)**. These are the markers of a life lived in the Spirit, and "against such there is no law."

I need to point out that many people misunderstand the concept of the law in the New Testament. There are 18 different laws mentioned, and it's important to know which one is being referred to. For example, we are free from the law of sin and death **(Romans 8:2)**, but we are not free from the law of the Spirit of life in Christ. The key is to walk in the Spirit, and in doing so, we naturally fulfill God's will without being bound by the legalistic rituals of the old covenant.

The law of liberty, as mentioned in **James 2:12,** is the freedom to live in the Spirit, to love one another, and to bear the fruit of righteousness. This freedom does not mean living in the flesh or indulging in sinful desires, but rather living in the fullness of the Spirit, where love reigns supreme.

In conclusion, walking in the Spirit is about living in the liberty Christ has provided—not through the external observance of rituals, but through the internal transformation of the heart. When we walk in love, joy, and peace, we live in the Spirit, fulfilling the law of liberty and bearing fruit that reflects God's character. As believers, we must continually choose to walk in the Spirit and not be entangled again in the flesh, allowing God's divine nature to flow through us.

## **Walking in the Spirit: Crucifying the Flesh and Embracing God's Will**

The Bible is clear in **James 3:11-12: "Doth a fountain send forth at the same place sweet water and bitter? Can the fig tree, my brethren, bear olive berries? Either a vine, figs? So can no fountain both yield salt water and fresh."** In the same way, our lives should not produce a mixture of righteousness and sin. When we allow envy, strife, and bitterness to take root, confusion and every evil work will follow. **James 3:17** reminds us that the wisdom from above is **"first pure, then peaceable, gentle, and easy to be intreated, full of mercy and good fruits, without partiality, and without hypocrisy."**

If we are to walk with God, we must do so in the Spirit. **Galatians 5:16** tells us, **"Walk in the Spirit, and ye shall not fulfil the lust of the flesh."** Lust—anything contrary to God's will—exists within the flesh, and no amount of education or human effort can eliminate it. If education could solve the problem, the prison system would have already done it. Instead, we must crucify the flesh daily, just as Paul declared in **Galatians 2:20, "I am crucified with Christ: nevertheless I live; yet not I, but Christ liveth in me."**

Lust and sinful desires, like weeds, keep resurfacing. No matter how much we wish we could "weed the garden" of our hearts once and be done, the reality is that the flesh will always fight against the Spirit. **Galatians 5:17** says, **"For the flesh lusteth against the Spirit, and the Spirit against the flesh: and these are contrary the one to the other: so that ye cannot do the things that ye would."** The constant tension between flesh and Spirit is what makes lukewarm Christians miserable—convicted by God but unable to fully do His will because they haven't committed to walking consistently with Him.

Here is a vivid illustration: imagine two people pulling you in opposite directions, each saying, "Walk with me!" One represents the way of the flesh, the other the way of the Spirit. It's impossible to walk in both directions. You'll be torn apart, unable to follow either path fully.

This is what **James 1:8** calls being **"double-minded,"** and such a person is unstable in all their ways.

This divided walk was also the issue with the Israelites during Elijah's time. They attempted to worship both Baal and the God of Abraham, Isaac, and Jacob, resulting in a spiritual drought that manifested as three and a half years of literal drought. Elijah confronted them in **1 Kings 18:21**, saying, **"How long halt ye between two opinions? If the Lord be God, follow him: but if Baal, then follow him."** Their double-mindedness led to God withholding the rain, not "global warming,".

In conclusion, walking in the Spirit requires complete surrender to God's will, crucifying the flesh daily, and avoiding the temptation to serve both God and the desires of the flesh. To walk with God is to walk in peace, joy, and righteousness, producing the fruits of the Spirit that align us with His will. As Jesus said in **Matthew 5:9, "Blessed are the peacemakers: for they shall be called the children of God."** Let us choose to walk wholeheartedly with Him, leaving behind the things that pull us away from His perfect plan.

## ** Walking in the Light: The Path of Truth, Obedience, and God's Commandments**

In the words of the Apostle John, **"I have no greater joy than to hear that my children walk in truth" (3 John 1:4).** Walking in truth means walking according to God's commandments, following His Word faithfully. I once had a long-running TV program was aptly named

*Walking In the Light*, a reflection of **John 8:12** where Jesus declares, **"I am the light of the world: he that followeth me shall not walk in darkness, but shall have the light of life."** This is the essence of living as a true believer—walking in obedience to the Lord's ways.

Jesus himself calls us to this walk of obedience, explaining in **2 John 1:6, "And this is love, that we walk after his commandments."** Love for God isn't just an emotion—it's demonstrated by living according to His will, aligning our lives with His commands. Walking with God is not a one-time decision; it is a continuous path of obedience. As Jesus says in **Matthew 7:14, "Strait is the gate, and narrow is the way, which leadeth unto life, and few there be that find it."** This narrow path is the path of obedience and trust in God's Word.

When we stray, repentance must come quickly. It is essential to recognize when we have stepped off the path and to ask God for forgiveness. The straight and narrow path doesn't allow for detours. Jesus is **"the Saviour of all them that obey him" (Hebrews 5:9).**

I have spent countless hours in discussions with individuals who resist these biblical truths, often unable to accept the importance of obedience. As **2 Corinthians 4:4** warns, **"The god of this world hath blinded the minds of them which believe not."** These individuals reject God's commandments, preferring their own ways over God's truth. I liken their behavior to that of picky children, only wanting to eat what they're used to, even when it's unhealthy. I have experienced trying to feed children nutritious meals, only to find they would refuse the balanced options in favor of unhealthy foods, like hot dogs. In the same way, many believers have been spiritually spoiled on "junk food"—teaching that offers comfort but lacks the depth and nourishment of God's full counsel.

Look at the analogy of feeding babies. At first, they resist the food that will help them grow, spitting it out, but with persistence, they eventually swallow what they need. Spiritually, it's much the same—people may resist the truth, but we must continue to share it, guiding them toward a life of walking with God.

Walking with God is not just a ticket to heaven; it is the safest, most secure path in a world growing darker by the day. We must walk with God out of reverence, not pride. **Proverbs 9:10** says, **"The fear of the Lord is the beginning of wisdom,"** and this healthy fear of the Lord keeps us walking closely with Him, especially in these times of uncertainty. Now, more than ever, it's crucial to walk in the light, following the truth, and obeying God's commands.

As the world grows more chaotic, the only sure place is in the arms of our Heavenly Father, walking with Him in faith, truth, and love. We are called to walk with God, to stay in the light, and to follow the path that leads to eternal life.

# How to Live in the Miraculous!

This is a quick explanation of how to live and move in the realm of the miraculous. Seeing divine interventions of God is not something that just spontaneously happens because you have been born-again. There are certain biblical principles and truths that must be evident in your life. This is a very basic list of some of these truths and laws:

1. You must give Jesus Christ your whole heart. You cannot be lackadaisical in this endeavour. Being lukewarm in your walk with God is repulsive to the Lord. He wants 100% commitment. Jesus gave His all, now it is our turn to give our all. He loved us 100%. Now we must love Him 100%.

*My son, give me thine heart, and let thine eyes observe my ways (Proverbs 23:26).*

*So then because thou art lukewarm, and neither cold nor hot, I will spew thee out of my mouth (Revelation 3:16).*

2. There must be a complete agreement with God's Word. We must be in harmony with the Lord in our attitude, actions, thoughts, and deeds. Whatever the Word of God declares in the New Testament is what we wholeheartedly agree with.

*Can two walk together, except they be agreed? (Amos 3:3).*

*For the eyes of the LORD run to and fro throughout the whole earth, to shew himself strong in the behalf of them whose heart is perfect toward him (2 Chronicles 16:9).*

3. Obey and do the Word from the heart, from the simplest to the most complicated request or command. No matter what the Word says to do, do it! Here are some simple examples: Lift your hands in praise, in everything give thanks, forgive instantly, gather together with the saints, and give offerings to the Lord, and so on.

   *I can of mine own self do nothing: as I hear, I judge: and my judgment is just; because I seek not mine own will, but the will of the Father which hath sent me (John 5:30).*

4. Make Jesus the highest priority of your life. Everything you do, do not do it as unto men, but do it as unto God.

*If ye then be risen with Christ, seek those things which are above, where Christ sitteth on the right hand of God. Set your affection on things above, not on things on the earth (Colossians 3:1-2).*

5. Die to self! The old man says, "My will be done!" The new man says, "God's will be done!"

*I am crucified with Christ: nevertheless I live; yet not I, but Christ liveth in me: and the life which I now live in the flesh I live by the faith of the Son of God, who loved me, and gave himself for me (Galatians 2:20).*

*Now if we be dead with Christ, we believe that we shall also live with him (Romans 6:8).*

6. Repent the minute you get out of God's will—no matter how minor, or small the sin may seem.

*(Revelation 3:19).*

*As many as I love, I rebuke and chasten: be zealous therefore, and repent.*

7. Take one step at a time. God will test you (not to do evil) to see if you will obey him. *Whatever He tells you to do: by His Word, by His Spirit, or within your conscience, do it.* He will never tell you to do something contrary to His nature or His Word!

*For whosoever shall do the will of my Father which is in heaven, the same is my brother, and sister, and mother (Matthew 12:50).*

*Then went he down, and dipped himself seven times in Jordan, according to the saying of the man of God: and his flesh came again like unto the flesh of a little child, and he was clean (2 Kings 5:14).*

## ABOUT THE AUTHOR

Dr. Michael and Kathleen Yeager have served as pastors/apostles, missionaries, evangelists, broadcasters, and authors for over four decades. Doc Yeager has authored over 350 books. They flow in the gifts of the Holy Spirit, teaching the Word of God with wonderful signs and miracles following in confirmation of God's Word. In 1982, they began Jesus is Lord Ministries International, Biglerville, PA 17307.

<u>Some of the Books Written by Doc Yeager:</u>

"Living in the Realm of the Miraculous #1"

"I need God Cause I'm Stupid"

"The Miracles of Smith Wigglesworth"

"How Faith Comes 28 WAYS"

"Horrors of Hell, Splendors of Heaven"

"The Coming Great Awakening"

## Dr Michael H Yeager

"Sinners In The Hands of an Angry GOD", (modernized)

"Brain Parasite Epidemic"

"My JOURNEY To HELL" - illustrated for teenagers

"Divine Revelation Of Jesus Christ"

"My Daily Meditations"

"Holy Bible of JESUS CHRIST"

"War In The Heavenlies - (Chronicles of Micah)"

"Living in the Realm of the Miraculous #2"

"My Legal Rights To Witness"

"Why We (MUST) Gather!- 30 Biblical Reasons"

"My Incredible, Supernatural, Divine Experiences"

"Living in the Realm of the Miraculous #3"

"How GOD Leads & Guides! - 20 Ways"

"Weapons Of Our Warfare"

"How You Can Be Healed"

**"To Many Books To Mention"**

Printed in Great Britain
by Amazon

f5a15520-4edf-4b78-addb-4e3f86e52ca4R01